YAR

TO BE A PILOT

TO BE A PILOT

5TH EDITION

DAVID BRUFORD

Airlife
England

The information contained in this book is believed to be correct at the time of publication. However, the author and publishers cannot be held responsible nor liable for action taken on this information. Terms, details and conditions are constantly subject to change by the relevant authorities. All material relating to the Private Pilot's Licence and associated ratings should be checked against the appropriate Civil Aviation Publication, *CAP 53*. All material relating to the Commercial and Airline Transport Pilot's Licence and associated ratings should be referenced against Civil Aviation Publication *CAP 54*. Matters relating to the tax concessions for *Piloting Transport Aircraft – Level 4 – NVQ Q1019882* should be considered against the Finance Act 1991 and subsequent amendments.

The process of Flight Crew Licensing (FCL) harmonisation between the Civil Aviation Authority (CAA), the European Community and the 32 (eventually to be 51) Joint Aviation Authority (JAA) member states continues. The information contained in this book details the current CAA legislation and the proposed JAA legislation up to the Notice of Proposed Amendment (NPA) FCL-1; JAR-FCL Part 1 (Aeroplane) Flight Crew Licensing Requirements (5th Draft) and NPA-FCL-3; JAR-FCL Part 2 (Helicopter) Flight Crew Licensing Requirements (4th Draft) and subsequent updates. The date required for implementation of the JAA requirements at the time of publication is 1 July 1999 for aeroplanes and 1 June 2000 for helicopters. The practicalities of JAA inspection of so many member states means that there will be an adoption process from 1999 (2000 for helicopters) and a transition period of three years after the implementation date. Up to the implementation date national licences will be issued, even if all training is within the JAA regulations. After the implementation date JAA licences will be issued.

This fifth edition first published in the UK in 1998
by Airlife Publishing Ltd.
First edition published 1982, second edition 1988, third edition 1991, and fourth edition 1996

British Library Cataloguing-in-Publication Data
A catalogue record for this book
is available from the British Library

ISBN 1 84037 081 5

Typeset by Servis Filmsetting Ltd, Manchester
Printed in England by Biddles Ltd, Guildford and King's Lynn

Airlife Publishing Ltd
101 Longden Road, Shrewsbury SY3 9EB

Preface

'Don't envy the birds, join them! If you can drive a car, you can fly an aeroplane!' Popular lines quoted encouragingly in advertisements of light aircraft manufacturers and flying schools. You have probably seen them, and perhaps wondered if it can possibly be true. Can anyone fly? Could *you* do it?

The answer is a qualified yes. Just about anyone can be taught to handle the controls of an aeroplane. Young children have done it, and so have elderly grandparents. Yet in truth the most commonly quoted parallel, that between driving and flying, is not really a valid comparison. Flying an aeroplane can actually be easier than driving a car. There is much less traffic to worry about for one thing. Nevertheless, flying does demand quite different skills, and levels of skill, to those required of the motorist. A pilot needs a co-ordination of mind, hand and eye which quite simply are not an inherent part of everyone's makeup. Just as a few people are 'natural' drivers or sports players, so many struggle to master even the basic rudiments, and some never do.

To put it very simply, a pilot needs a good car driver's co-ordination and reflexes, a horserider's sense of balance and subtle touch of hand, a sailor's eye for weather, and much else besides. It is possible to teach almost anyone the basic mechanical ability to control an aeroplane in flight, but not everyone can hone that skill to the level necessary to become a safe and proficient pilot.

This is not intended to be a textbook for those wishing to learn how to fly. There are many excellent training manuals on the market which deal with the subject. This book's purpose is to whet the appetites of aspiring private and professional fliers and, I hope, to help answer those questions: **'Could I do it? Could I fly? Do I have what it takes to be a pilot?'**

BUCKINGHAM PALACE.

There is no accounting for taste and there is even less accounting for the choice of occupation. Some people may develop a burning ambition to fly at a very early age, others may find it unappealing at best and positively frightening at worst. Unfortunately, ambition does not necessarily go with aptitude. Lucky are the people who find that they have a natural aptitude for the one thing they desperately want to do.

In theory, flying an aeroplane is no more difficult than driving a car. In practice flying an aeroplane is more like steering a boat. A car is, or should be, permanently connected to a road; aircraft and boats operate in the fluid media where the condition of the weather is a far more critical factor for a pilot than for a driver.

For anyone with the ambition, or the obsession, to take up any occupation, it is always a good idea to find out as much about it as possible before becoming too committed. This book is designed precisely for this purpose. Having read it, I think it is worth your while to bear in mind that a flying career is much more than just a meal-ticket with fringe benefits. You will find an endless challenge in all aeronautical matters; that you are constantly having to cope with new equipment, new techniques and new concepts. Most important of all, you will find that you have got to keep on top of a flying job both for your own peace of mind as well as for the safety of the people who put themselves in your care.

Foreword from First Edition

Contents

Acknowledgements

For their help in supplying information for Mike Jerram's first, second and third editions of *To be a Pilot*, thanks go to Air Cdre C. A. Aldose, CB, DEC, AFC, MA, secretary to The Air League Educational Trust; the British Airline Pilot's Association; Capt Graham Jenkins, former manager of Flight Crew Resourcing at British Airways; the Flight Crew Licensing and Information and Publicity departments of the Civil Aviation Authority; Danny Forman, MBE, chief executive of the General Aviation Manufacturers & Traders Association; Miss Hazel Prosper, Corps Director of the Girls Venture Corps; Jack Nicholl, Peter Latham and Colin Beckwith, past principals of Oxford Air Training School; James Gilbert, editor of *Pilot*, for permission to adapt certain material which first appeared in the magazine; Flt Lt Larry Chamberlain of HQ Air Cadets, RAF Newton; Sqn Ldr G. L. Margitta, BA, RAF, Royal Air Force College Cranwell; the staffs of the Army, Royal Air Force and Royal Navy Careers Offices; and the public relations staff of British Airways, British Aerospace, and RAF Strike and Support Commands.

For their assistance in producing the amendments and additions for the revised edition, thanks go to Bob Fielding (Lt RN Retired); Lt-Cdr P. J. Hardy RN; Pauline Harris, Brian Marindin, CFI, and CPL/IR instructors at Airways Flight Training, Exeter; Chris Martin; Julia Hines of the Cabair Group; Scott Brown, FAA Gatwick; Peter Moxhan, marketing manager, Oxford Air Training School; Mike Beeston, CFI, Exeter Air Training School; Maj (Retired) R. A. James MBE, Headquarters, Director Army Aviation, Middle Wallop; Tony Hines, Aviation Training Association; Public Relations Office, HQ Air Cadets, RAF Newton; Wg Cdr Alan Watson and Sqn Ldr David Cuthbertson, Headquarters University Air Squadrons, Royal Air Force College, Cranwell; David Snelling of the British Airways press office; Minesh Patel of the British Airways Flight Operations Training Centre, Heathrow; Captain Peter McKellar, CAA Examiner.

David Bruford
November 1998

Chapter 1
About Aeroplanes

Whatever your eventual aim in aviation, to fly simply for pleasure as a private pilot, to become an airline pilot, or even a fighter pilot, your basic tool will be the same – an aeroplane. Every would-be flier's introduction to flying is likely to be in a small training aeroplane.

Most flying schools in Britain use either American or French aircraft. The types most likely to be encountered at any typical flying school are the high-wing Cessna 150, 152 and Aerobat, the low-wing Piper Tomahawk, Cherokee, Cadet and Warrior and Gulfstream Cheetah and Tiger from the USA, and French Robins. All are similar in concept, being two- or four-seaters with side-by-side seating, fixed tricycle undercarriages (with a nosewheel at the front) and four-cylinder horizontally-opposed piston engines in the 100–180 hp range. There are flying schools which operate tail-wheel aircraft for training, and, should you wish, it is still possible to learn to fly in vintage open-cockpit aeroplanes such as the de Havilland Tiger Moth, which first began training pilots over half a century ago.

Let us look at one of the most common training aeroplanes, the Cessna 152. The high-wing layout is not everyone's favourite, because the wings restrict the pilot's vision overhead and when turning, but in a downward direction visibility is good. Conversely, in a low-wing type such as the Piper Cadet upward visibility is less restricted, but the wings obscure a substantial part of the downward view. Aircraft with large clear canopies, such as the Robin 200 and 400 and Slingsby T.67, provide the best compromise, but it is still a case of swings and roundabouts. Each type has its champions. In common with all conventional aircraft, the Cessna 152's airframe comprises three primary elements: the fuselage, which contains the cockpit or cabin area; an engine, in this case a 108 hp Textron-Lycoming O-235 mounted at the front of the fuselage; and flying surfaces – the wing and tail group. These in turn have movable control surfaces which, when used in various combinations, direct the movement of the aircraft in the air.

First, look at the tail group. The horizontal surface is known as the tailplane or, in US parlance, the horizontal stabiliser. Its hinged rear portions are known as elevators. Some aircraft have tailplanes which move in their entirety, popularly called 'stabilators'. Elevators control the aircraft in the pitch axis. Imagine the aeroplane from the side (profile) view. Its centre of gravity (cg) is roughly at a point one quarter to one third back from the forward (leading) edge of the wing. Now imagine an axis or shaft passing through that point from wingtip to wingtip. In pitch the aircraft will pivot about that axis, nose-up or nose-down, and the hinged elevators control the direction of that movement. By raising the elevators using the control wheel or stick, a downward force is created on the aircraft's tail in flight, thus raising the nose, and vice versa. Inset into one elevator is a smaller hinged surface called a trim tab. Its function is to relieve the pilot of the control force needed to hold the elevators at any desired angle, to trim the aeroplane at a selected pitch angle. It is moved by a small wheel in the cockpit, and the tab moves in the opposite direction to the desired elevator movement: trim tab down, elevator up; trim tab up, elevator down.

The fixed vertical tail surface is called a fin, or vertical stabiliser in US parlance. Its rakish angle or sweepback is more for reasons of styling than for aerodynamic purposes. The hinged rear surface of the fin is the rudder. Its function is to control the aeroplane in its yaw or normal axis. Let us return to our cg point, but this time imagine the aircraft in plan view, as seen from directly above, with the axis or shaft passing vertically through its cg. Now imagine the nose of the aeroplane swinging from side to side as it revolves around the axis. That is yaw, and it is controlled by the rudder, which is moved by a pair of pedals.

Now look at the Cessna's wings. At the end of each wing is a narrow hinged surface called an aileron. Unlike the elevators on the tailplane, which move in unison, the ailerons move in opposition. That is, as one goes up, the other goes down, and they control the aircraft in its roll axis. Returning to the side view, this time the shaft passes through the aircraft from nose to tail. Picture the aircraft head-on, in front view, and imagine one wing dipping, rotating the aeroplane about the shaft. This is called rolling, or banking, and is governed by the ailerons via control wheel movement.

Inboard from the ailerons are two larger surfaces called flaps.

Unlike the elevators and ailerons, flaps do not raise above the fixed surface to which they are attached. They lower and retract back flush with the wing surface. Their purpose is to provide additional lift to the wing by altering the camber (curvature) of its aerofoil surface. They also create drag and act as aerodynamic brakes for slow flight or during the landing approach. Flaps can be manually operated through a simple mechanical linkage, as in the Piper PA-28, or electrically activated, like those on the Cessna 152.

Now we will climb aboard to view the Cessna's cockpit. There are two seats, side-by-side, the interior is not too generous on room for large-framed occupants. Ahead is the instrument panel and, projecting from it, dual control wheels. 'Wheel' is something of a misnomer, because they are not round on most modern aircraft, but shaped like one half of a spectacle frame, or like a flattened letter 'W', and are often called control yokes. Some training aircraft, usually those of British or European origin, still have the conventional control column, floor-mounted and hinged at its base, a 'joy-stick' in the old Royal Air Force jargon, but 'wheels' are much more common. They are mounted on shafts which slide in and out of the instrument panel, and the wheels also rotate, car-style, though over a much more limited 'lock-to-lock' range. They do not, however, steer the aeroplane on the ground, as most student pilots discover on their first flight when they turn the wheel energetically and wonder why the aeroplane refuses to follow their command.

The control wheel moves the elevators (back for up, forward for down) and the ailerons (wheel to the right to bank right, and vice versa). The rudder is controlled by a pair of pedals mounted in the foot well. Pushing on the left pedal applies left rudder and yaws the aircraft to the left, while right pedal gives right rudder and right yaw. The system is logical but not entirely natural. At first, many student pilots feel a strong urge to try to slew the aircraft left or right as they would a soap-box go-cart, using exactly the opposite of the correct sense of rudder pedal movement. The rudder pedals are usually linked to a steerable nosewheel which is effective when the aircraft is on the ground. Steering when taking off, landing and taxying is accomplished with the feet, using both rudder and nose-wheel. The rudder pedals may also operate brakes on the aircraft's main wheels, though some trainers have hand-operated brakes, and all have a parking brake. On aircraft fitted with toe-brakes, pressure on the top of the rudder pedals operates the brakes, either in unison or individually (to assist in making a tight turn while taxying or parking, for example). They are sensitive, and require much lighter pressures than the brake pedals in most family cars.

Remember the trim tab? It is operated by a trim wheel, which may be set on a central console or between the seats, as in the Cessna 152, or in the cabin roof area in the form of a hand crank, as on some Piper Cherokee models. Trim wheels operate in the natural sense, forward movement of the wheel to trim nose-down, backwards to trim nose-up. They are marked with a neutral position, when the trim tab trails flush with the elevator surface.

Other controls?

There is a fuel selector that may have a simple on/off movement to allow the fuel to flow from the tanks in the wings, or it may be selectable to individual (left/right) tanks as required. In simple high-wing aircraft such as the Cessna 152, fuel is fed to the engine by that most reliable force, gravity, so there are no fuel pumps to concern us. On low-wing types an electric fuel pump is used to ensure a constant flow of fuel during engine starting, take-off and landing. An engine-driven fuel pump provides a reliable fuel supply in cruising flight.

There are three principal engine controls. The throttle sets the required power, much like the accelerator pedal in a car, except that when flying you do not have to make constant adjustments as you might when driving. Once the desired power setting has been selected, it is left until a change in flight configuration, such as a climb or descent, demands a new setting. The throttle is hand-operated and can take the form of a simple push-pull knob or a quadrant-mounted 'power lever'. Whichever type the aircraft has (the Cessna 152's throttle is the push-pull type), the throttle control operates in the natural sense, forward to increase power, back to reduce it. A friction nut or collar is provided which is tightened to hold the power setting required.

The mixture control, readily identified by its red knob, controls the fuel/air mixture reaching the engine. During training flights it will most usually be found in the rich (fully forward) position. Leaning out the mixture (reducing the fuel/air ratio) confers greater fuel economy and smoother running at altitude, but will not concern the student during the earliest training flights. When the mixture control is pulled fully back (out from the instrument panel) it is in the 'idle cut-off' position, and the engine will be starved of fuel and will soon stop. Mixture controls are moved to idle cut-off only when the aeroplane is on the ground and parked, or during airborne or ground emergencies when cutting off the flow of fuel to the engine may be necessary – hence the cautionary red knob.

Another knob operates a carburettor heat control. This is used to provide heated air to the carburettor and prevent ice forming in the carburettor intake. If ice is allowed to develop, a loss of power can result, so heat is applied at regular intervals as a preventive measure. Carburettor icing can occur under certain quite common climatic conditions in the UK. Carburettor heat controls again may take the form of push-pull knobs or levers. Unlike throttle and mixture controls, carburettor heat knobs are pulled out to function (hot air) and pushed in for off (ambient temperature air).

Supplementary to these primary engine controls, but no less vital, is a magneto switch, marked 'off-left-right-both' for the engine's dual ignition system. Each magneto is tested before flight, but the 'both' position is used at all other times, and the magneto switch usually doubles as a starter switch by turning the aircraft's ignition key past the 'both' position to start, just like a car. There is a plunger-type primer for priming the aircraft's engine before starting, usually necessary only when the engine is cold.

What about those banks of instruments?

Airliner cockpits have dozens of instruments seemingly spread over every available piece of cockpit wall and roof, although these are increasingly being replaced by electronic flight instrumentation system (EFIS)* cathode ray tube (CRT) displays in the 'glass cockpits' of new-generation transport aircraft. Such aircraft also have two or three highly trained crew members to monitor their instrument displays. A light training aeroplane's instrument array is much more modest.

There are three main types of instruments on the panel: flight instruments, engine and system instruments, and navigational instruments. We will look at each group individually.

The flight instruments are: airspeed indicator (ASI), altimeter, artificial horizon, vertical speed indicator (VSI), turn-and-slip indicator and direction indication (DI). Although it is included in

*Many words and phrases in aviation tend to be abbreviated. This book, therefore, contains many such instances. To assist the reader, and to avoid the need to read back through sections of text, a full glossary of abbreviations is provided on page 143

this section on flight instruments, the direction indicator is primarily a navigation instrument that indicates the aircraft's heading in degrees magnetic against a compass card, and does not influence the control of the aircraft.

The airspeed indicator gives the aircraft's indicated airspeed in miles per hour or knots (nautical miles per hour). That is speed through the air, not over the ground. The ground speed varies according to whether the aircraft is flying into a headwind or gaining the benefit of a tailwind. The airspeed indicator works by measuring the static pressure of (still) air surrounding the aircraft and comparing it with the dynamic (moving) pressure of air moving past the aircraft.

The altimeter also measures air pressure. It is essentially an aneroid barometer with an adjustable subscale which is pre-set to a known pressure value. In training you will soon become acquainted with two common pressure settings identified by the 'Q' Codes QFE and QNH.

The Q codes are a form of abbreviation once commonly used in air-to-ground communications in the days of wireless telegraphy. Their use is now mostly restricted to aviation and a few other usages. The QFE is the local airfield pressure setting that will cause the altimeter to read zero when the aircraft is on the ground at the airfield. The QNH is a sea-level pressure setting that will make the altimeter indicate the airfield's elevation (height above sea level) when the aircraft is on the ground. Altimeters are calibrated in feet, with the adjustable sub-scale graduated in millibars, inches of mercury or hectopascals. An altimeter works on a pressure differential, giving altitude above sea level (QNH) or above the elevation of the airfield whose local pressure (QFE) has been set. It does not tell you your height above the ground over which you are flying. Consequently if you fly over a hill which is 1,000 ft high with an altimeter reading 1,500 ft on the sea-level (QNH) pressure setting, your altitude will be 1,500 ft above sea level, but your height (or vertical clearance) above the hill is only 500 ft.

The vertical speed indicator measures the rate of pressure change as the aircraft climbs or descends, and presents this information as a feet-per-minute up/down reading. The pressure instruments – ASI, altimeter and VSI – all suffer from a slight lag in displaying information when airspeed, altitude or rate of climb or descent change. Inexperienced student pilots often find themselves impatiently chasing these instruments, making further corrections instead of waiting for the instrument indications to stabilise.

The artificial horizon operates on the gyroscope principle. It provides information about the aircraft's attitude relative to the horizon. The instrument's face comprises a replica aeroplane symbol combined with a horizon bar which moves to show the aircraft's relative position; climbing, diving, banking left or right, or in any combination. This instrument forms the basis of instrument flight when no outside visual references are available.

The turn-and-slip indicator, also commonly known as the turn and bank indicator or turn co-ordinator, is a two-part instrument comprising a needle, or in more modern turn co-ordinators a miniature aeroplane, that deflects left or right as appropriate when the aeroplane banks into a turn. The other part of the display is a free-floating ball inside a spirit level. The ball remains centred when the aircraft is in a balanced or co-ordinated turn, but moves sideways if the aircraft is slipping (sliding sideways into the direction of the turn) or skidding (slithering outwards away from the direction of the turn).

The engine and system instruments in a small training aeroplane such as the Cessna 152 are few and quite straightforward, usually comprising a tachometer or rev counter that indicates engine revolutions per minute, oil temperature and oil pressure gauges, an alternator gauge that measures electrical load (like an ammeter in a car), and a suction gauge that monitors suction for the vacuum-driven gyroscopic instruments. Fuel quantity gauges are fitted to show how much fuel remains in the aircraft's petrol tanks, but as a prudent pilot you will always make a visual check of each tank's contents before flying, and monitor fuel consumption during each flight.

The most common navigation instrument is still the old-fashioned magnetic compass. This is usually a bubble-type instrument mounted high up on top of the instrument panel glareshield or in the upper part of the windscreen. Magnetic compasses are slow in responding to an aircraft's directional changes, and are subject to acceleration errors and regional magnetic influences. For these reasons a direction indicator or directional gyro is used for more precise navigation. However, the DI must be synchronised with the aircraft's magnetic compass before take-off and at regular intervals throughout a flight.

Later, in more advanced training, students will encounter two further navigational instruments, the automatic direction finder (ADF) and the VHF omnidirectional range (VOR) receiver. The ADF is a radio compass whose indicator needle points to the position of a ground station transmitter to which it is tuned. The VOR receives signals from ground stations which transmit their signals along each of the 360 degrees of the compass, or 'radials' as they are known. By tuning to a ground station within range and selecting a desired radial, a pilot can fly directly to, or away from, the station by keeping an indicator needle centred in the instrument display.

What about radio communications?

All modern training aircraft have a very high frequency (VHF) transceiver for communicating with airfield control towers and other air traffic control ground facilities. Some basic aircraft are equipped with cabin speakers for listening and a hand-held microphone for speaking. For training aircraft, individual headsets with boom microphones are preferable because they permit exchanges between pupil and instructor to be heard easily through an intercom facility. Headsets offer the additional advantage of effectively excluding some engine and airflow noise which unfortunately is an all-too-noticeable feature of light aeroplanes. When wearing a headset the pilot transmits to ground stations by pressing a 'push-to-talk' switch conveniently set into the hand-grip of each control wheel.

Does it still sound daunting? Probably, if you are entirely unfamiliar with aeroplanes. However, rest assured that it will all seem much clearer when you see the aircraft's controls and instruments actually working. If you are still game to try, and you should be, read on.

Chapter 2
The Private Pilot

The minimum basic licensing requirement for flying powered aeroplanes without supervision is the Private Pilot Licence, popularly called the PPL. It is broadly equivalent to a full driving licence, permitting the holder to fly private aeroplanes for personal business and pleasure and to carry passengers provided no payment is received. A PPL (Aeroplanes) or PPL (Helicopters) is therefore the starting point for nearly all non-commercial civilian flying except gliding, hang gliding and microlight flying. These have their own systems of pilot qualification and are outside the scope of this book.

No general academic qualifications are required to qualify for the issue of a licence and there is no lower age limit at which you may start learning to fly. However, to apply to be cleared to fly solo while training you must be at least 17 years of age under the CAA rules but this will change in July 1999 under the JAA rules, when the age drops to 16. Under either set of rules you must be 17 before a licence can be issued. At the other end of the age scale there is no upper age limit. Many people in their sixties and seventies have successfully completed PPL training courses.

Unlike the driving licence, which can be obtained by taking any haphazard form of tuition that will get an applicant through the test, a PPL is granted only after completion of a recognised syllabus of ground and flight instruction conducted by properly qualified flying instructors, and after successful passes have been obtained in ground examinations and flying tests. Although a pilot friend or relative can probably give you some basic experience at the controls of an aeroplane, such experience cannot be counted towards the minimum number of hours required for the PPL course unless he or she is a qualified flying instructor.

The licensing of pilots in the United Kingdom is the responsibility of the CAA, whose records show that there are approximately 27,500 active PPL holders in the country, with some 3,800 new licences being issued annually. At the time of writing the CAA is in the process of harmonising the UK's rules with those of the European Community and Joint Aviation Authority (JAA) member states. These rule changes are due to come into force on 1 July 1999, so for the PPL and all other licences and rating the current CAA requirements will be shown together with the 1999 JAA requirements.

The CAA syllabus for the PPL currently calls for a minimum of 40 hours of flying instruction. From July 1999, however, this will be increased to 45 hours in line with the JAA requirements, the other changes being that five of these training hours may be in a synthetic flight trainer, which is a type of ground based electronic flight simulator. These 40 and 45 hour figures are simply statutory minimum requirements, and do not guarantee that a licence is automatically granted on completion of those hours. In practice, the average qualifying time for students is some 55–60 hours of instruction, a fact to keep in mind when calculating the likely cost of obtaining your licence.

So you think you would like to become a private pilot? What to do? Where to go?

There are more than 200 flying schools, clubs and training organisations in the United Kingdom. They vary in size from chummy one-man, one-aeroplane businesses to large operations with fleets of a dozen or more aircraft, staffs of full-time instructors on call seven days a week and comprehensive facilities on the ground for classroom study.

What you are taught should not vary, because the training syllabuses, examinations and tests are standardised. How you are taught, the rate at which you progress, how much you pay, and whether you get good value for your money will depend on wise selection of your training school, and probably on a bit of luck. Big does not necessarily mean best, nor small, cheapest. A one-man outfit might provide a very personal touch, but consider what may happen to the continuity of your training if that one man goes sick, or his one aeroplane is grounded for a prolonged period of maintenance.

How do you go about choosing?

A selection of clubs and flight schools are listed in the Contact Address Section at the back of this book. The Aircraft Owners and

Pilots Association (AOPA) publishes an annual directory of their member clubs, and a very comprehensive 'Where to Fly Guide', containing courses offered, aircraft fleets, membership costs and flying charges, is published annually in the March issue of *Pilot* magazine. Even your local *Yellow Pages* may offer some suggestions.

As a first step, obtain one of these lists and search out the operators in your area. How far you cast your net is up to you. Do not assume that the school nearest you must be the one to choose. An airfield and a flying club within a mile or two of your home that might appear ideal at first consideration, but be warned that much of your training will involve general flying in clear airspace. If your 'local' airfield is a commercial airport with its own protected airspace, you will have to spend time at the beginning and end of each lesson flying to and from a practice area. This could be good experience, but it will cost you money in flying time during which you will not be progressing through the exercises of the PPL syllabus. At a busy airport you may also find yourself frequently waiting in a line of aircraft waiting to take off. Since charges for flying lessons are often costed from engine start to engine stop, or 'brakes off' to 'brakes on' in flying jargon, this can be a very expensive and unproductive traffic jam. Airfields where many flying clubs and schools operate will also create traffic problems when it comes to the 'circuits and bumps' part of the PPL course. During this part of the training you will spend many hours doing nothing but repeatedly taking off, flying around the rectangular course of the airfield's circuit, landing, and taking off again.

At a busy airfield other aircraft may seriously limit the number of circuits which can be flown in an hour's lesson. On the other hand, a busy airfield environment with a mix of commercial and private traffic will quickly breed confidence in radio and air traffic procedures.

Having selected likely airfields within your reach, list the training establishments at each and pay them a visit. Do not be daunted if the airfield entrance is dotted with 'keep out' or 'pilots only' signs threatening dire peril to trespassers. They are only there to keep out small and inquisitive children. Weekends are invariably busy if the weather is reasonable, and therefore are a good time to gain an impression of flying school activity, but you may not get the fullest attention from staff when they are busiest. A weekday visit would probably be better for asking questions, getting an escorted tour of the facilities and looking over aircraft.

Flying is still very much an enthusiast's activity in Britain. An increasing number of flying clubs and schools, perhaps the majority, do have plush, sparkling premises with smartly-dressed staff, airy classrooms and comfortable lounges. However, more than a few still operate from buildings left behind by the Services after the war, with facilities sometimes little improved in the meantime. Whether you select a small homely club or a large flying training school is largely a matter of personal preference.

You can learn a great deal from your reception on your first visit. For a start, does anyone bother to ask if they can help you? Flying does generate legendary *camaraderie* among fellow pilots, but sad to say strangers are not universally accorded warm welcomes, even from those very people whose business it is to win over new customers. If your reception is too offhand, go somewhere where they do want your business. Otherwise, explain that you think you might like to learn to fly and ask if someone can answer a few questions. Prepare your questions in advance, ideally written down, and write down the answers you receive. Pilots and instructors tend to talk in abbreviations and jargon, so do not be afraid to ask for an explanation of anything that appears to be expressed in a secret language.

You should ask how many training aeroplanes they have. This can be very important. If there are just two in the fleet, for instance, the chances of lessons being delayed or cancelled through technical faults or because the last pilot did not return the aircraft on time can be very high. Ask if the school has its own, or readily-available, maintenance facilities to ensure aircraft reliability and availability. How many instructors are there, and what is the student:instructor ratio? Is there an efficient system for booking lessons that will ensure you get the instructor you want?

Flying instruction is not a well-paid profession at private pilot level. As a result, the instructional staff at many clubs and schools is made up of young aspiring professional pilots building hours towards their Commercial Pilots' Licences. There is nothing wrong with this practice, except that it results in a rapid turnover among instructors, which in turn leads to discontinuity in training. An occasional change of tutors can be refreshing, but having a different instructor for every lesson is a frustrating and expensive business, because you might find yourself going over some parts of the PPL course many times while never touching others. It is unlikely that many schools could guarantee one-to-one instruction from the same instructor throughout a PPL course, but one which has a good number of older full-time professional flying instructors on staff should score highly on your list of possibilities. Ask also how many training staff are Qualified Flying Instructors (QFIs), and how many are Assistant Flying Instructors (AFIs). Bear in mind that after 1999 there will be a transitional period where the ratings of AFI and QFI are due to be replaced with one rating of Flying Instructor (FI). QFIs are the more experienced and are essential to 'sign you off' at certain stages of the syllabus, such as your first solo, so check carefully how many are on the staff and how often they are available.

Ask to see the ground training facilities. Are there proper classrooms, lecture rooms, or at least individual briefing cubicles for study and for pre- and post-flight discussions with your instructor? Does the school run classes, in the evenings or at weekends, for the PPL examination subjects? Ground school is just as important as flying on the road to gaining a PPL. There is nothing worse than trying to master complex theory or solve a tricky navigational problem in a noisy office with a telephone ringing or in a club bar surrounded by chattering pilots, beeping video game machines and demented one-armed bandits.

Note also whether the whole operation is run in an efficient and businesslike manner. Are the premises and aircraft clean and well cared for? It is reasonable to assume that a seedy and run-down operation may adopt a similarly careless attitude to your training. You may get your licence eventually, but it will have cost more and taken longer than it should have done.

Try to talk with other students at the school. Ask what they think of it, and how they have progressed with their training. Do not believe everything you hear. Every activity has its share of professional moaners who can find fault with everyone and everything, but a high number of complaints should be taken as a warning that all may not be well.

Trial lessons

Most flying schools offer trial lessons, and you should take advantage of this, at least at those schools which seem to meet all other requirements. Do not be alarmed at the term 'trial'. It is flying that is on trial, not you. The purpose of the flight is, or certainly should be, to acquaint you with the sensations of flight in a small aircraft and to demonstrate the basic effects of the aeroplane's controls, not to decide whether you have the makings of a pilot.

A trial lesson, sometimes called an air experience flight, usually lasts about 30 minutes. The cost can run from £50 up to £145 depending on the package. The schools with the lower costs usually carry out the flights on a subsidised basis, hoping that the student will become hooked. Most provide a basic ground briefing followed by about 30 minutes in the air. To get the most out of the experience it is best to prepare in advance, and *The Trial Flight Guide*, available from flying shops or direct from Airlife Publishing Ltd, gives a good explanation of what will happen ahead of the great day.

Acorne Sports Ltd have put together a package that enables you to purchase a voucher redeemable from any of 45 flying schools in the UK. With the voucher they supply a list of participating schools, and for an extra £14 include a clipboard, log-book, pen, introductory audio-cassette and student pilot membership to AOPA, the pilot's association.

Two types of voucher are available. The 'Discovery' voucher at £75 provides a 30-minute introduction to flying and 30 minutes in the air. The 'Explorer' voucher at £139 also offers the introduction to flying, but increases the air time to about an hour and includes a landing away from the flying school's home base. Details can be obtained from Acorne Sports Ltd, Wycombe Air Centre, Booker, Marlow, Buckinghamshire SL7 3DR. Telephone: 01494 451 703 or fax (for credit card orders) on 01494 465 456.

However you go about booking your trial flight, a considerate school will arrange your first light aeroplane trip on a calm day with good visibility, free of gusting winds, turbulence or low clouds which are not good introductions to flying. The lesson should be a preflight briefing on what you are going to do in the air, followed by a practical introduction to aviating with you handling the controls under the instructor's supervision. If you get no more than a sightseeing ride with the instructor remaining steadfastly silent and not relinquishing the controls for a moment, suspect the worst of the school concerned.

Several facts will quickly emerge during your trial flight. Flying in a light aeroplane is not at all like riding in the claustrophobic confines of a large airliner. You will fly much lower and enjoy a fine panoramic view of the world denied to those who can only peer through the few square inches of an airliner's window. You will also discover, however, that the cockpits of two-seat training aeroplanes are noisy and often cramped, which makes them poor classrooms in which to absorb theory and further emphasises the need for proper ground study facilities at the school, where your instructor can brief you in peace and quiet. The use of headsets with an intercom overcomes some of the problems of effective instructor/student communication, and reduces the fatiguing effects of engine noise.

Still keen to become a pilot?

Now is the time to talk to your selected school about booking a course of lessons for the PPL syllabus. Because of the number of hours needed to qualify for a PPL varies among individuals, most schools provide flying tuition by the hour, rather than signing up students for a complete course from the outset. Some offer fixed-price courses, so check first to see if it is a guaranteed get-your licence deal. It may be that the course fee includes only the statutory minimum of 40 hours (or JAA 45 hours) flying, which will almost certainly not be enough. Otherwise you pay as you go, usually at an hourly rate, or *pro rata* against the time from an engine start to engine stop. Dual flying – flight time with an instructor – usually comes a little more expensive than solo use of an aircraft, typically by a few pounds more per hour, though many schools now adopt a higher 'training' charge rate throughout a course, irrespective of whether the student is accompanied by an instructor or flying solo.

How much will it cost?

Hourly charges vary from school to school, for different aircraft, and in different geographical locations. In 1996 a typical hourly charge for dual instruction in a Cessna 152 or Piper Tomahawk class of aircraft, including VAT, was about £70, but it can be considerably higher in the London area, for example. On the assumption that it will take some 55 hours to complete the course, a sum of £4,000 should therefore be regarded as the likely cost of the flying element of a PPL course. Add medical examination fees, the cost of books, maps and ancillary equipment, examination and flight test charges and the licence issue fee, and £4,500 is a realistic assessment of a total outlay. You will find PPL courses offered for much less, but, whatever rate you are quoted, do determine exactly what the charge includes. Schools have been known to attract business by offering seemingly generous hourly rates while neglecting to point out that they do not include such non-optional extras as preflight briefings, instructor's time, airport landing fees and VAT.

Some schools will arrange personal loans through finance

companies to pay for flying tuition. Many also accept popular credit cards for payment, and it is not totally unknown for understanding bank managers to offer loans. It is worth asking a school if they give discounts for block bookings, such as 10 hours instruction paid for in advance. In general, however, parting with too large a sum in advance is not wise. It is possible that you may decide to give up before completing the course, or, as has happened to a number of unfortunate students, the school could go out of business. Payments by credit card can protect you from suffering a loss, as if the school does cease trading the credit card company will, within certain conditions, reimburse you. However, from the school's point of view they will be unable to offer much of a discount if they have to pay a significant percentage of their profit to the card company.

You may be asked to become a member of the school or club. This is a normal insurance prerequisite for flying their aeroplanes, and takes the form of a one-time joining fee and annual subscription which entitles you to use all the club's facililties and join in social activities. Most clubs also offer family or social membership for spouses, children and friends that enables them to fly as passengers in club aircraft. Apart from flying, you will find that most clubs and schools also have social activities, and many have a bar, strictly for after-flying drinking!

Regarding insurance, do check that the operator holds appropriate aircraft and liability cover which indemnifies you against claims if you are unfortunate enough to have an accident or incident while flying. Do not be afraid to ask to see their current policy and aircraft certificates. Nowadays the policy wordings are in 'plain English' so it should be relatively easy to check that all pilots flying club aircraft are covered for public and passenger liability. A reputable school will be happy to provide evidence of cover. This is very important. Even a minor accident on the ground can cause very expensive damage to an aircraft. A crash involving other people, aircraft or property could result in potentially ruinous claims. If you have a personal accident policy or intend taking out a life assurance policy after you have taken up flying training, be sure to tell the company that you are learning to fly. Otherwise the policy will contain a clause excluding cover while the policy-holder is in an aircraft except as a fare-paying passenger, or words to that effect. Cover for private flying can usually be obtained for a very small increase in premium. If your insurance company tries to tell you otherwise, look for another one. Life policies taken out before you intended taking up flying are unaffected.

Are you fit enough to be a pilot?

Although you do not have to meet any medical standards before starting to learn to fly, before you can fly a powered aeroplane solo, and consequently before you can obtain your PPL, you must have a valid medical certificate which doubles as a Student Pilot's Licence. It is strongly recommended that you obtain a medical certificate before you commit yourself to a full PPL course. This will avoid the possible frustration of going through the expense and training up to the level of your first solo and then discovering that you are unable to pass the medical.

Contrary to popular myth, you do not have to be super-fit astronaut material to become a pilot. Airline and military pilots are required to maintain very high levels of physical fitness which are constantly monitored, but the Class III medical certificate currently needed for a PPL sets much less demanding standards. To obtain a medical certificate you must undergo an examination by a doctor authorised by the CAA to carry out such tests. Your local general practitioner cannot conduct the examination unless he or she is a CAA Authorised Medical Examiner (AME). However, there is a good geographic spread of AMEs throughout the country. Most large towns have one, and your flying school can probably give you a list of those practising in the local area. Some larger airports have facilities for a medical to be carried out 'in house' with an AME making regular visits to the airport surgery. Appointments may usually be booked through the main flying club based at the airfield.

The straightforward medical examination has to be paid for at the time, and fees vary according to the doctor and depth of examination required. You will first be asked to complete CAA Medical Form 46 and a personal health questionnaire detailing significant medical conditions from which you may have suffered. Although the relevance of some questions may not be apparent, the form should be completed as full and truthfully as you are able. The doctor will check eyesight, hearing, reflexes, respiratory system and blood pressure, among other things. For applicants aged 40 years or over, a resting electrocardiogram (ECG) is required, usually necessitating a hospital visit.

If all is well, your Medical Certificate will normally be issued straightaway. A Class III certificate is valid for five years for those aged 40 (or up to age 42 if issued close to the 40th year), two years for those 40–50 years old, one year for 50–70-year-olds, and for six months after the 70th birthday. The ECG examination is required for renewal of the certificate every four years between the ages of 40–50, every two years between 50–60 years, annually between 60–70 years and every six months for those over 70 years. A further condition requires that any certificate holder must have an ECG within two years of passing their 40th birthday, whatever the date of expiry of their current certificate.

All licensed pilots must hold a current medical certificate for their licence to remain valid, and must inform the CAA in writing of any injury or medical condition that might invalidate the certificate. Women should note that, in the event of pregnancy, the medical certificate is automatically invalidated for the first 13 weeks and from the 27th week until the actual birth. Solo flights are allowable during weeks 14 to 27, providing all anti-natal checks are attended satisfactorily and any abnormalities are reported to the doctor. If any complications develop, the CAA must be informed. After the birth a medical report is required, and providing this is satisfactory the CAA will issue a 'fit letter' reinstating the full privileges of the medical certificate.

Anyone in good health and of average fitness should have no problem passing the PPL medical examination. Certain complaints such as epilepsy, diabetes requiring medication for control, and cardiac problems normally preclude the granting of a medical certificate. For this reason, and because some disqualifying conditions may not be known to the would-be-pilot, applying for a medical certificate before starting training is essential. Eyesight defects which are correctable with spectacles or contact lenses are usually acceptable. If the vision is outside specific parameters without glasses, the medical certificate will probably be endorsed with a requirement for the holder to carry a spare pair of spectacles when flying as a precaution againsts loss or breakage in the air.

Under JAA proposals expected to be in force by July 1999, the need for a CAA Class III medical will be replaced by the requirement that the student, and potential PPL holder, holds a valid JAA Class 1 or Class 2 medical certificate. On the assumption that no student will bother with the JAA Class 1 medical at this stage, only the Class 2 requirements are listed. The JAA medical certificate is valid for five years for those aged under 40, two years for under 50s, one year for those aged 50–64, and six-monthly for those aged 65 and over. Under JAA rules, an ECG is required before the issue of your first medical certificate, not just after age 40, and a further ECG is required every two years for those aged 40–49, annually for 50–64-year-olds and six-monthly for the 65 and overs. JAA regulations accept that dual training may be undertaken by a student without a medical certificate being held, but a valid Class 2 medical certificate is required before first solo.

The loss of limbs or other physical impairment does not automatically exclude one from becoming a private pilot. Many paraplegics have successfully gained their licences, and there is an annual sponsorship scheme detailed in this book that provides PPL training for the disabled. The CAA requirement is that a disabled pilot must be able to operate all of the aircraft's controls fully. Adapted aircraft controls such as those which enable the rudder to be operated by hand instead of by the feet, may be acceptable provided control movement is not restricted. Quick-conversion kits to modify aircraft for disabled pilots have been developed for many common training types. The CAA Medical Branch examines each disabled applicant for a PPL medical certificate on merit. Far from being ogres, the staff are most anxious to assist anyone with medical problems to get into the air if it is possible within the constraints of safety.

The PPL Course

We have already noted that the CAA course for the PPL until 1999 is of a minimum 40 hours duration. It must be conducted to a syllabus which has been recognised by the CAA and comprises an integrated programme of flying and ground tuition. The school or club is required to keep detailed records of each student's progress to ensure that training has been carried out systematically.

Full details of the United Kingdom PPL syllabus is contained in the CAA booklet CAP 54 – *The Private Pilot's Licence and Associated Ratings*, which is essentially reading for any aspiring PPL. Briefly, the recognised syllabus calls for a minimum of 20 hours dual instruction, including four hours each on pilot navigation and instrument flying and a minimum of ten hours of solo flying. This must include at least four hours cross-country flying as a pilot-in-command during the nine months preceding application for a licence. This must encompass a cross-country flight visiting two aerodromes, one of which must be at least 50 nautical miles from the home base.

Private Pilot's Licence – Aeroplanes – CAA requirements (up to 1 July 1999)		
PPL(A) 40 hr flight time minimum	20 hr dual instruction	4 hr pilot navigation
		4 hr instrument flying
		2 hr stall/spin awareness and avoidance
	10 hr solo flying, pilot-in-command and unaccompanied	
	4 hr cross-country as pilot-in-command, including a flight that visits and lands at two aerodromes, one of which must be at least 50 nautical miles from the home base	
	6 hr in any of the above	

The CAA Flight Training Syllabus is divided into a sequence of numbered exercises:

1. Aircraft familiarisation
2. Preparation for and action after flight
3. Air Experience
4. Effects of controls
5. Taxying
6. Straight and level flight
7. Climbing
8. Descending
9. Turning
10. Slow flight, stalling, stall awareness and avoidance training
11. Incipient spinning, spin awareness and avoidance training
12. Take-off and climb to the downwind position, engine failure after take-off
13. The circuit, approach, landing and going around
14. First solo flight
15. Advanced turning
16. Operation at minimum level
17. Forced and precautionary landings
18. Pilot navigation, compass turns and map reading; solo navigation flight test; qualifying cross-country flight
19. Instrument appreciation and flying

All of the exercises then culminate in the General Flight Test (GFT). You will have noticed exercise 14, first solo flight, that unrepeatable moment, the high point of every pilot's life, from novice to airline captain, when first you are in sole command of an aeroplane. When will you go solo? When your instructor thinks you are ready, and not before. You must hold a medical certificate before you go solo, and most flying clubs will insist that you pass the air law examination, which is a sensible safety requirement. Most students are sent off on their first solo circuit of the airfield when they have completed 10–12 hours of dual instruction. There is no set time in the syllabus, and the figure will vary depending on an individual's aptitude. Contrary to popular belief, going solo does not mean that you have gained your wings and become a pilot. Far from it. It is a confidence-building exercise which assures you that your instructor has faith that you can take-off, fly around the airfield circuit pattern, land and cope with any likely emergencies which might occur. Nothing more. Just when that golden moment comes and you write 'first solo' in your pilot's log book (usually in unnecessarily large and shaky handwriting) depends mostly on your own ability and rate of learning, so take no notice of 'experts' who tell you that unless you go solo in 'x' number of hours you stand no chance of gaining your licence. You may be sure that if you go on too long before showing signs of reaching solo standard your instructor will tell you.

The JAA PPL

The JAA PPL requirements, expected to come into force from 1 July 1999, are very similar except that the flight time is increased to 45 hours and five of these hours can be flown in a ground-based flight trainer or simulator. The cross-country flight wording is also amended, but in practice has virtually the same requirements.

The requirements for fixed amounts of navigation and instrument flying are replaced by an amended syllabus. Exercises 1 to

<table>
<tr><th colspan="3">Private Pilot's Licence – Aeroplanes – JAA requirements (from 1 July 1999)</th></tr>
<tr><td rowspan="5">PPL(A)

45 hr of flight time minimum</td><td colspan="2">Up to 5 hr may be on a flight navigation procedural trainer or flight simulator approved by the authority</td></tr>
<tr><td colspan="2">10% of total flight time as pilot-in-command, up to a maximum of 10 hours, may be credited towards the 45 hours by holders of pilot licences for helicopter, microlights (having fixed wings and movable aerodynamic control surfaces acting in all three dimensions), gliders or self-sustaining gliders or self-launching gliders.</td></tr>
<tr><td colspan="2">25 hr dual instruction</td></tr>
<tr><td>10 hr supervised solo flight time</td><td>5 hr solo cross-country flight time, including a flight of at least 150 nautical miles that visits and lands at two aerodromes</td></tr>
<tr><td colspan="2">The balance of hours if not claimed on a simulator or trainer, or by existing licence holders, must be made up of supervised solo flight time or dual instruction</td></tr>
</table>

15 are identical to those in the CAA training schedule, but exercise 16, operations at minimum level, is replaced by forced landing without power, and exercise 17 follows the list again with precautionary landings.

It is at exercise 18 that the real changes occur. This exercise is split into three parts, A, B, & C. A & B fall in with the CAA course, with B covering the operations at lower level. In 18C, radio navigation and en route radar is covered. This gives the student the opportunity to receive basic training in the navigation systems that would, under the CAA system, only be covered if the qualified PPL holder went on to take further instrument flying training. The final exercise, 19, covers instrument appreciation under both the CAA and JAA systems, but only to a level of safe flight on instruments, not navigation.

The CAA's Navigation Flight Test (NFT) and GFT are replaced by just one JAA 'skill test'. This must be completed within six months of the completion of training and the time cannot be used towards the minimum hours. This tests the student's abilities plus at least 60 minutes of navigation testing, although this, if agreed between the student and the flight examiner, may be flown as a separate test. The skill test is broken down into five sections, including the navigation test. If a student fails more than one section, the whole test must be taken again. If only one section is failed that particular section may be taken again, but if the re-test is failed, or if while getting to the re-test section the student fails one of the previously passed sections, the whole test has to be taken again. All of the sections must be passed within a six-month period, but there is no limit to the number of skill tests that can be attempted, although if the student fails to pass all sections in two attempts, further training, as determined by a 'competent authority', will be required.

How long will the PPL course take?

Again, this depends on many factors, perhaps most important of which is the frequency of the lessons. Continuity is vitally important in any learning process, in none more so than in flying, and in the early stages it will certainly determine how quickly you go solo. Long gaps between lessons will invariably mean spending a period of each detail relearning something forgotten from the previous session. This will inevitably increase the duration and cost of the entire course.

If possible, try to fly at least once a week, preferably more fre-

Cessna 150s and 152s are popular two-seat trainers, widely used by British fying schools. (Mike Jerram)

All-composite construction Slingsby T67M Firefly II, used by a number of PPL and Commercial schools for basic and advanced flying training.
(John Dignan, Slingsby Aviation)

Instrument panel of Cessna 172, typical of modern light aircraft cockpits. (Cessna)

Cessna 172 Skyhawk is the world's best-selling light aircraft, used for training and touring by many flying schools. (Mike Jerram)

American Piper Warrior (above) and French Robin 400 (below) are four-seaters, equally suited to training and touring. (Mike Jerram)

Glider towing may be performed by holders of Commercial Pilots Licences. It is one way or building flying hours and experience. (Mike Jerram)

A Night Rating is often the first 'step up' for private fliers after gaining their PPLs. (Mike Jerram)

quently. Best of all, if you can set aside a period of two or three weeks, flying each day as weather permits, you can probably cover a substantial portion of the syllabus quite quickly. Bear in mind, though, that flying instruction and all light aircraft operation is very weather dependent. The UK student who does not have a few lessons cancelled because of unsuitable conditions either has a bad memory or is incredibly lucky. It is frustrating, but you will have to learn to live with it. Aeroplanes also have a habit of developing niggling faults just as you are about to fly. It is therefore inadvisable to try to fit a flying lesson into a day on which you have a busy programme of work or social commitments. Rather, set aside an entire day and schedule several lessons, with time between each for ground study of the exercises to be flown. You can help keep the school's schedule running smoothly by always arriving in plenty of time for preflight briefings from your instructor and for checking the aircraft before flying. If you have to cancel for any reason, do try to give as much advance notice as possible, so that the aeroplane and instructor can be allocated to another student. Next time it could be you waiting to fit in another hour's flying.

Some flying schools offer full-time residential courses for the PPL which aim to complete the course within a few weeks. This is an excellent idea, provided you can spare the time and money, with the caveat that the British weather is an unwelcome and often unco-operative intruder into the best-organised courses.

Ground School

The Ground Training element of the CAA PPL syllabus covers the following technical subjects:

- **a** Air legislation
- **b** Navigation
- **c** Meteorology
- **d** Principles of flight, airframes and aero engines, airworthiness and aircraft instruments
- **e** Aircraft type (the specific model of aeroplane used in your training)
- **f** Human performance and limitations.

The 1999 JAA PPL syllabus seems shorter:

- **a** Air law
- **b** Aeroplane general knowledge
- **c** Flight performance and planning
- **d** Human performance and limitations.

It looks shorter because navigation and meteorology have been included under flight performance and planning, giving you one two-hour exam instead of three of one hour each. Ground training, or ground school, is an important and statutorily required part of the PPL syllabus. It must be closely co-ordinated with flying training so that the relevant subjects and procedures have been discovered on the ground before they are put into practice in the air. In practice, a considerable amount of study will be needed to prepare for the PPL examinations, which must be passed before a licence is issued. Again it is difficult to put a precise figure on the time needed as it varies according to the student's ability to learn, but 50–100 hours is accepted as an average figure.

Although pre- and post-flight briefings from your instructor should be an essential part of each flying lesson, few flying schools offer one-to-one teaching for the ground examinations, unless you are prepared to pay for an instructor's time to give you individual tuition. Most offer lecture courses for groups of student pilots, often conducted as evening classes, for which a separate, usually modest charge is made. Audio-visual courses using video and aural tapes are also employed. Some polytechnics and further education centres may also offer tuition, and a few schools run week-long or weekend intensive ground school courses covering the entire PPL ground school syllabus, including sitting the technical examinations, with on-site accommodation if required. A number of home study courses are also available, including audio tapes covering all of the PPL subjects; these can be put to good use in the car tape player during long journeys, or while travelling to and from the airfield for lessons.

Your progress through the PPL course will be monitored by the school. The CAA recommends that schools issue students with copies of their syllabus which they can sign upon completion of each phase of training, agreeing that the items have been covered. You will also keep a record of your flying hours in your Personal Flying Log Book, which every student must submit with the licence application at the end of the course. Your log book is an important document – the only official record of your flying time – which must be maintained throughout your flying life.

The Tests

Before you can apply for a PPL you must pass written and oral examinations and take practical tests. The examinations consist of written papers on the technical subjects: airframes and engines, aviation law, flights rules and procedures, navigation, meteorology, human performance and limitations, and an oral technical quiz on the specific aircraft type on which you have trained. The written examination questions are of the multiple-choice type, e.g. *Flaps are fitted to aircraft to: a) Increase lift and drag while lowering stalling speed, b) Increase drag, payload and stalling angle, or c) Increase lift, drag and stalling speed.* The correct answer is *(a).*

The technical examinations and oral test are usually taken at your flying school. Under the CAA rules an hour is allocated for completion of each subject, with a minimum pass mark for each paper of 70%. Under the JAA rules the pass mark is 75%, with 90 minutes allowed for air law, 120 minutes each for aeroplane general knowledge and flight performance and planning, and 30 minutes for human performance and limitations. You do not have to sit all the examinations at once, you simply take each one when you feel you are sufficiently knowledgeable. Those that you fail have to be re-sat, and there's no limit to the number of times you can re-take each one. The CAA recommends that aviation law and flight rules and procedures should be passed before making the first solo flight, and those for navigation and meteorology (and flight radiotelephony if taken as a separate test–see below) before making the first solo cross-country flight. The JAA makes no particular recommendation, although your flying school will probably suggest that you pass all but human performance and limitations before you go solo. All theoretical tests must be completed within a twelve month period, and the pass results will be accepted towards the grant of a PPL during the 36 months from the date of successfully completing the examinations.

The practical tests for the CAA course comprise the NFT and GFT, the latter being the final hurdle before the issuing of your licence.

The NFT comprises a flight of about 1½ hours duration over a triangular route, during which an examiner assesses the student pilot's flight planning; handling of air traffic control instructions; dead reckoning navigation, map reading; ability to maintain course, altitude and airspeed at normal and low levels; ability to establish position visually after disruption of the planned flight; and to carry out a practice diversion to an alternative destination in simulated poor weather conditions. The NFT is a pass or fail test, all elements of which must be successfully completed in a single flight, or the test has to be retaken. Once the NFT has been completed you can make your qualifying solo cross-country flight. This consists of a triangular journey with two landings at airfields away from base, one of which must be at least 50 nautical miles from your starting point. Controllers at the airfields visited sign a landing card to confirm your visit, and are also invited to observe and comment on circuit discipline and landing procedure.

The GFT as its name implies, examines the student's competence in the exercises of the PPL flying syllabus, any (or all) of which you may be asked to demonstrate to the examiner's satisfaction during a flight lasting about an hour. Should you fail, the examiner will advise you of those aspects of your flying which need refining, and after some further dual instruction and practise, you can take the GFT again. The JAA skill test, which replaces the GFT and NFT, should last about 2 hours and has five sections covering the same standards, except that the use of radio navigation aids must be demonstrated and radar headings, provided they do not cause the flight to enter cloud, may be accepted.

Most larger flying schools have a CAA-delegated examiner on staff, usually a senior instructor or the CFI, so unlike the driving test you do not have to apply months in advance to take your PPL GFT.

For student pilots, learning to fly also means mastering the use of the aircraft's VHF radio transmitter for two-way communication with airport control towers and other air traffic control facilities on the ground. Radiotelephony (RT) training is an integral part of the PPL syllabus, and leads to a test for the issue of a Flight Radiotelephony Operator licence, popularly known as the RT Licence, which is a separate document to the CAA and JAA PPL.

A student pilot must therefore learn the language of aviation. Not the 'bandits at five o'clock, angels one-five, over and out' banter of the movies, but the precise language of air traffic control, which has two functions: to convey the maximum information in the fewest words, and to avoid ambiguity which could lead to a misunderstanding and result in an accident.

'Affirm' is substituted for 'Yes', 'Negative' for 'No', and the phonetic alphabet, A-alpha, B-bravo and so on, is used when anything needs spelling out or abbreviating to initials. Once you overcome microphone nerves and learn to relax you should slip into the correct phraseology without stumbling over your words. Books and cassette tapes are available to teach RT technique. You might also find an airband VHF radio useful for tuning to airport and

ATC frequencies to get the feel of radio procedures. A written examination and practical RT test, again usually conducted by your flying school, must be passed before an RT licence is issued. However, it is more usual for an instructor's certification of practical in-flight RT training and assessment of competence to be accepted in lieu of the practical test, avoiding the need for the separate tests.

The Licence

Once you have completed your CAA or JAA PPL course, technical examinations, qualifying solo cross-country flight, skill test or navigation and general flight test, your examiner will send off your examination results, Personal Flying Log-Book and PPL application form to the CAA, which will enter a Certificate of Test in your logbook and return it with your brand-new PPL.

The licence, a computer-generated fold-out sheet in a plastic wallet, is non-expiring and yours for life. However, to maintain the validity of the licence, or 'keep it current', as we say, you must revalidate it by complying with various criteria. With the CAA PPL you need a Certificate of Experience entered in your log-book, confirming that you have completed a minimum of 5 hours flying experience in the 13 months preceding each 'signing off'. Of the 5 hours, at least three must have been logged as pilot-in-command without supervision. The remainder may be as pilot-in-command under supervision (PIC/US) with a qualified instructor or authorised examiner on check flights or tests, or dual flying instruction with a qualified instructor provided that at the end of the flights the instructor signed your log-book to certify your competency to fly unsupervised.

In practice, 5 hours of flying in 13 months is not enough to make you a safe or proficient pilot. If you do not fly as pilot-in-command for a period of more than 26 months you must undergo further training and take another flight test to revalidate your licence.

The privileges of the JAA PPL include the 'recency' rule. This means that the holder of the licence cannot carry passengers and act as pilot-in-command unless within the preceding 90 days he or she has made three take-offs and three landings as the sole manipulator of the controls (in simple terms, to be exclusively in control) in an aeroplane of the same type or class. Besides this, a revalidation, or renewal, of the JAA licence will be required every 24 months. This entails a proficiency check by making a one-hour flight (not a test) with a flying instructor and being able to prove that at least 12 hours has been flown, with at least 6 hours as pilot-in-command, in the 12 months before the expiry date. If these conditions cannot be complied with, the licence holder can take a Revalidation Test with an instructor, which, if passed, revalidates the licence for another 24 months. For holders of other ratings where an annual or biannual flight test is required, the proficiency check can usually be included as part of the flight test.

The validity of both types of PPL also depends on possession of a current medical certificate. If your certificate expires, or you fail a renewal examination, your PPL automatically becomes invalid until a medical certificate is reissued.

Many non-fliers suppose that a PPL gives you the right to fly any aircraft. This is sensibly not so, and your first PPL provisions are quite specific. If, as is most likely, the licence is issued for Group A, and termed a PPL(A), you may fly only single-engine landplanes weighing less than 5,700 kg. That allows a broad range of aircraft types which you could, in theory, fly quite legally. However, in practice, if you are hiring aeroplanes from the club or school where you learned to fly, you are likely to be restricted to the aircraft type on which you trained, or something very similar in terms of performance, complexity and handling, until you have gained more experience. Insurance premiums, or the availability of cover, are also likely to impose similar constraints even if you buy your own aircraft.

There are other restrictions to the basic PPL. You may not fly in airways-designated airspace effectively forming the 'motorways' of the air traffic system. You must remain in sight of the earth's surface, not in or above cloud, and with a minimum in-flight visibility of between 3 and 10 kilometres, dependent upon various criteria. The detailed privileges and exemptions applying to the PPL are many, and cannot be listed in depth here. CAP 53, *The Private Pilot's Licence,* gives the fullest information and should always be consulted for specific details.

Can you carry passengers?

Certainly, provided they do not pay you an element of profit for your services as a pilot and under the JAA PPL licence you comply with the 'recency' rule. The PPL is strictly an amateur licence in the literal sense, specifically forbidding flying for 'valuable consideration', although the acceptance of awards or prizes in amateur flying events such as races or rallies is permitted. Cost-sharing between a pilot and no more than three passengers is within the licence privileges if all, including the pilot, pay an equal share. Personal business users can legitimately pay the full costs of a trip from a personal or partnership business account, and an employee can claim reimbursement from an employer without such payments being considered illegal.

You can fly abroad with a PPL. The CAA licence is widely recognised, and the JAA licence (will be) more so. If you are flying a British-registered aeroplane there should be no problem operating in foreign countries provided you comply with all the necessary customs, immigration and air traffic procedures. If you want to hire a foreign-registered aeroplane while abroad, you will need to validate your British PPL for the country in question. This should be done in advance, since the time taken can vary from a few minutes' form filling to six months negotiation, depending on the country with which you are dealing. You will probably have to take an examination in local air law and have a check-ride with the operator hiring you the aeroplane. When all member states eventually comply with all JAA edicts there should be even less problems, as all European aircraft will be JAA registered, allowing any JAA PPL holder to fly it without problems. Even if not required by law, a check-ride or briefing of local customs will be well worth paying for.

Check-rides are also necessary in Britain if you want to hire an aircraft from a club where you and your experience level are not known. This may also be a requirement at your local club if you have not flown recently. Just how recently you must have flown varies from club to club. Some insist on a check-out with an instructor, which you must of course pay for, if you have not flown within a month, so there is a further spur to keep in regular flying practice.

Helicopters

The foregoing summary of private pilot training is directed principally at those seeking to learn to fly fixed-wing light aeroplanes for the issue of a PPL (Aeroplanes).

Learning to fly from scratch on helicopters is, however, possible, for the PPL (Helicopters). The CAA course duration is currently a minimum of 40 hours, as with fixed-wing aircraft, and the examinations and testing requirements are also identical, although certain items of the flying syllabus vary to incorporate those exercises specifically related to rotary-winged flight and to omit manoeuvres. Stalling, for example, cannot be performed in helicopters. As with the PPL(A) syllabus, the minimum hours are to be increased to 45 hours with effect from June 2000 under the JAA regulations. These hours are to be made up of 25 hours dual instruction, 10 hours of supervised solo time which includes at least 5 hours of solo cross-country time, and one cross-country flight of at least 100 nautical miles during which landings at two separate aerodromes are made. The balance of hours is made up of other specified training, with 2 hours claimed by the successful completion of a 'skill test' which will be the JAA equivalent of the current CAA GFT. Under current legislation the CAA permits holders of aeroplanes licences (except Group D microlights) to reduce the mimimum experience requirement to 35 hours on helicopters if they are adding a PPL(H) to their qualifications. A similar 5 hour reduction also applies to helicopter pilots seeking a fixed-wing PPL. Under the JAA rules a maximum of 5 hours may be credited towards the 45 hours for flight simulator training or by holders of pilot licences for aeroplanes, three-axis microlights, microlight helicopters, gyroplanes, gliders or self-launching gliders. The other main change is that the PPL(H) applicant must hold a valid JAR Class 1 or 2 medical certificate, as opposed to the current CAA requirement of a Class 3 certificate. The JAA ground school examinations are similar to the existing requirements, and are given the titles air law, helicopter general and type related knowledge, flight performance and planning (general and type related), human performance and limitations, and radiotelephony.

Helicopter flying training schools are becoming increasingly common. The cost of helicopter operation is much greater than that for light aircraft, although the popularity of light piston-engine helicopters (particularly the two-seat Robinson R22, which is widely used for rotary-winged training in the UK) has helped reduce the cost of obtaining a PPL(H). At 1996 rates you could expect to pay around £200 per hour for instruction on a Robinson R22, and at least twice that figure for flying a turbine-engine Bell JetRanger.

Training abroad

Recent years have seen a tremendous increase in the number of companies offering overseas 'package' training courses. These are mostly based in the USA, and to a lesser extent in France, where more dependable weather can increase the chances of completing a PPL course within a specific period, typically three to four weeks.

Two British operators offer courses in France (see page 131), based at Sisteron and Carcassonne. The advantage that these offer over most of the American schools is that their courses lead to the granting of a British CAA PPL, rather than an American Federal Aviation Administration (FAA) certificate, so you return fully qualified to fly in the UK. It is also possible on these courses to undertake the ground school part of the course and take the CAA examinations before going to France to start the practical side of the syllabus, freeing more time for cramming those vital 40 flying hours into three weeks. Some students have successfully completed the course in two weeks.

The attractions of the USA for taking a PPL course are principally cost and weather. Flight training and aircraft hire are much cheaper in the USA than in the UK or mainland Europe, so it is possible for operators to offer packages that include ground and flight training, exams, accommodation, return airline fares and sometimes car hire for figures that may be below the cost of flight training alone at home. Typical rates being quoted by US package operators in 1996 were around £1,300 for a basic PPL course, or £2,500 inclusive of accommodation, flight tickets and insurance.

US schools popular with overseas students tend to be in the southern states, Florida and Texas being particularly popular because there is a good chance that the weather will be suitable for flying on most days. This ensures that rapid progress should be possible, and completion of the course is quite feasible within three or four weeks; perhaps less if you learn quickly. Pick the right school and instructor, have good luck with the weather and everything should go as advertised.

It sounds too good to be true, but there are drawbacks. For the most part these courses are for a US FAA licence, not British CAA PPL. You will need an FAA medical certificate before you go, but this can be acquired in Britain. A list of FAA Appointed Medical Examiners can be obtained from the FAA office at Sipson Court, 595 Sipson Road, Sipson, West Drayton, Middx. UB7 0JD. Requests for the list should be made in writing to the above address, or by fax on 0181 754 8826, but *not* by telephone. Your FAA PPL can be validated for use in the UK when you return home, and you may continue to fly quite legally. However, the FAA requires pilots to take a biennial review (this is not required by the CAA, but will be under the JAA rules), which means that you will either have to seek out a UK-based FAA-designated instructor (and there are some) or return to the USA for your check-ride when the time comes round.

The alternative, which is probably wiser, bearing in mind that American and British air traffic control systems and operating procedures differ considerably, that our airspace is generally much more congested and restricted, and that the clear blue skies of Florida are no preparation for British weather, is to convert your FAA PPL to a CAA one. The CAA is prepared to do this providing you can meet certain requirements. First you must send in the FAA Temporary Airman Certificate which will have been issued by your examiner in the USA, your medical certificate, log-book and a fee for assessment by the flight Crew Licensing Branch at Gatwick Airport. If all is well, you must then sit the UK Air Law examination, take an RT test and pay for the issue of your British licence. Ground tuition at a UK school will probably be necessary preparation for the examinations and tests. You would be wise also to take some dual flying instruction to familiarise yourself with UK procedures. If you plan to hire aircraft from a British club or school, they will almost certainly require this anyway. All of this will add to the cost of getting your PPL in the USA, but it does give you valid licences for both countries; a great asset if you plan to take holdays or do further training or experience-gathering in America.

While most operators offering package courses abroad are honest and endeavour to provide a good service, there have been sorry instances of students finding themselves having to pay substantially for hidden 'extras' after arriving in the USA, or discovering that promised accommodation or training was not up to standard. As most of these operators require full payment in advance of your travelling to the USA, you would be well advised to make careful enquiries of any school whose offers you are tempted to accept. At the very least ask for a list of satisfied British students who have trained at the school, and contact them for their experiences. If a school cannot or will not provide such a list, go elsewhere. Also check exactly what you are getting for your money. Are State taxes, examination fees and insurance indemnity included? If car hire is offered, does it include the cost of a collision damage waiver?

Some courses guarantee to get you your licence for the quoted fee, no matter how many flying hours it takes. However, if, for whatever reason, you fail to complete the course in the three weeks or whatever you have booked, you will have to bear the cost of flying back to America at some future date to complete the course. On this point, remember that to obtain your Temporary Airman Certificate before leaving the UK you must pass the written examinations, whose results can take some time to come through unless they are taken at an FAA exam centre which uses a computer-based testing system providing 'instant' results. There is also a 30-day wait to re-sit failed parts of the exam, though this can be and often is waived. You must also pass your check-ride or practical test (equivalent to the CAA NFT and GFT), after which the Temporary Airman Certificate is issued by the examiner. Without written and check-ride passes you will come home with no more than some good flying experience.

Since the air fares included in package courses are usually on non-amendable tickets, you will either have to fly back again at your own expense or stay on and bear the cost of a one-way air ticket to complete the course.

The prospect of learning to fly in clear blue skies, warm sunshine and with sandy beaches nearby may seem attractive, but remember that becoming a pilot, particularly in as short a period as three or four weeks, will be hard work, and there is unlikely to be much time for anything other than studying, flying, eating and sleeping. Wherever you choose to learn to fly, it should be enjoyable, but do not expect it to be a relaxing holiday.

Another 'overseas' possibility, much closer to home, is training in the Channel Islands. They are free of VAT and have lower rates of duty on aviation fuel, so it is possible to learn to fly there for less than at some schools on mainland Britain. Operators on Guernsey and Jersey offer residential courses for the CAA PPL and ratings and include various grades of accommodation as desired. Their PPL courses generally last three to four weeks and include ground school.

Moving up

As we have seen, the PPL is a minimum qualification. Its scope can be greatly expanded as experience grows by a number of additional 'ratings' which are briefly described below.

Night Rating

A private pilot who possesses only a basic PPL cannot legally fly as pilot-in-command (PIC) after dark when carrying passengers. For post-sunset flight with passengers a Night Rating is required. The minimum experience requirement for application for a CAA PPL Night Rating is 50 hours total flying time, of which 20 hours must be as PIC, with a minimum of 5 hours instrument flying instruction. At least 10 hours of this PIC time must have been gained since making an application for the PPL(A). The Night Rating course consists of a minimum of 5 hours night flying, including five solo night flights with take-offs and landings, and may be taken before the necessary 50 hours minimum has been achieved (though the rating cannot be granted until the minimum qualifications have been gained), making a Night Rating a practical step worth considering shortly after qualifying as a PPL. The CAA Night Rating is non-expiring if five solo night circuits and landings have been completed as pilot-in-command within the proceeding 13 months.

Private Pilot's Licence – Night Rating – CAA requirements (up to 1 July 1999)		
PPL(A) with 50 hr total flight time	20 hr pilot-in-command	10 hr pilot-in-command since making an application for a PPL
	5 hr instrument flying instruction	
	5 hr night flying to include five solo take-offs and landings	

The JAA PPL Night Rating allows for 1 hour less instruction but includes the recency rule for the carriage of passengers. The issue of the rating requires a PPL holder with 5 hours night flying to include five solo take-offs and landings. The instruction is for 3 hours of dual night flying and 1 hour night navigation. As with the CAA rating, it is non-expiring, but to carry passengers you must have made three take-offs and three landings while exclusively in control of the aircraft, at night, within the preceding 90 days.

Private Pilot's Licence – Night Rating – JAA requirements (from 1 July 1999)		
PPL(A)	5 hr night flight time	3 hr dual instruction in night flying
		1 hour of night navigation instruction
		5 solo take-offs and landings at night

IMC Rating

IMC stands for instrument meteorological conditions. As we have seen, the basic PPL restricts the holder to operating within sight of the earth's surface and to a minimum flight visibility for flight without passengers outside controlled airspace. The PPL syllabus provides a measure of instrument flying instruction aimed at giving a student limited ability to control his aircraft and to perform simple manoeuvres by sole reference to instruments. This training, however, is no more than basic insurance against inadvertently entering cloud or poor weather conditions, hopefully enabling the pilot to retain control while returning to a point where visual reference to the ground can be regained. The IMC Rating is the minimum qualification for private pilots seeking to operate in instrument meteorological conditions, though it does not give a free hand to fly on the Airways system or in controlled airspace, for which a full Instrument Rating (see below) is normally required. Exercising the privileges of the rating is also restricted to UK airspace only. It is not recognised in any other country, and is a rating exclusively available to a British PPL holder. The future of the IMC Rating is in doubt at the time of publication. Pressure to harmonise with the JAA member states by 1 July 1999 is strong, but the UK's negotiating team may well achieve a special dispensation for the IMC Rating, or its possible replacement, the Instrument Weather Rating (IWR) to be retained after this date. In any event, you would be hard pushed to find a British pilot, instructor or examiner who believes the rating should be dropped, and its existence will be maintained for as long as possible.

To qualify for an IMC Rating a pilot must have logged a minimum of 25 hours flying in aeroplanes gained after applying for a PPL, of which at least 10 hours must have been as PIC, including not less than 5 hours on point-to-point cross-country flights, and must hold a valid R/T Licence. The IMC Rating course consists of a minimum of 15 hours dual instrument flying training, of which 2 hours may be conducted on a simulator; a ground training course; a written examination and a flight test.

Instrument Meteorological Conditions Rating – Aeroplanes – exclusively a UK CAA rating		
PPL plus 25 hr experience	10 hr pilot-in-command	5 hr cross-country
R/T licence	15 hr IMC instruction	2 hr may be on a simulator

Although the IMC Rating may not be issued until the minimum experience qualifications have been met, the flight and ground school courses may be taken in advance, and some students do proceed directly to the IMC Rating course upon completion of their PPL training.

The flight training syllabus for the IMC Rating consists of a Basic Stage, comprising instrument appreciation and basic and intermediate flight manoeuvres on instruments, with limited and partial panel flight, and the Applied Stage, which covers pre-flight planning, departure and en route flying, instrument let-downs and approaches, and bad-weather circuits and landings. PPL holders who have current Night Ratings are exempt from 3 hours of the Basic Stage of the IMC Rating syllabus. The Flight Test, which lasts for approximately 1½ hours, requires the pilot to demonstrate the ability to navigate on radio aids while flying solely by reference to instruments, to make a pilot-interpreted instrument approach, and to show ability to use a second type of instrument approach aid, either pilot- or ground controller-interpreted. The full syllabus is detailed in CAP 53. The IMC Rating is valid for a period of 25 months after a successful flight test, which may be completed in more than one flight, but not more than three, and the entire test must be completed with a 28-day period. The ground training syllabus, for which a minimum of 20 hours study is recommended, covers physiological factors, aircraft flight instruments, the use of Aeronautical Information Publications, flight planning and the privileges of the IMC Rating. The written examination consists of one paper which includes questions covering the planning and execution of a typical flight under instrument flight rules (IFR) operating outside controlled airspace. The flight test and written examination must be passed within the 12-month period preceding an application for an IMC Rating, but there is no specified maximum duration for the course of instruction, although a concentrated IMC Rating course should last six to eight days.

The Instrument Weather Rating

At the time of publication a proposal is being put forward for the IMC rating to be replaced by the Instrument Weather Rating (IWR). This will grant similar privileges but require a slightly increased amount of training. Twenty hours' instrument weather flying instruction will be required, of which 6 hours may be on an approved flight training device. There is also a requirement for at least 50 hours ground training followed by a 2 hours written exam which has a 75% pass mark. The various types of ground instruction are shown in the table below. The training must be completed within an 18-month period, but at least 20 hours training must have been completed in the 12 months before taking the flight test. The rating, which can be applied to a PPL or Basic Commercial Pilot's Licence, will contain the same 'recency' rule relating to passengers as the PPL, and will be renewable every 12 months.

<table>
<tr><th colspan="3">Instrument Weather Rating – Aeroplanes</th></tr>
<tr><td rowspan="6">PPL (with 30 hr logged since applying for a PPL) plus 20 hr instrument weather flying instruction of which up to 6 hr may be in an approved flight training device</td><td>2 hr VHF Omnidirectional range navigation training</td><td rowspan="4">Out of this group a maximum of 4 hr may be simulator training</td></tr>
<tr><td>2 hr non-directional beacon training</td></tr>
<tr><td>1 hr standard instrument arrival and standard arrival training</td></tr>
<tr><td>2 hr approach system training hours instrument</td></tr>
<tr><td colspan="2">5 hr cross-country route flying</td></tr>
<tr><td colspan="2">8 hr instrument weather flying instruction which may include any of the above</td></tr>
</table>

Multi-Engine Rating

In its basic form, the PPL covers only Group A aeroplanes (single-engine landplanes). To be able to fly as PIC of a multi-engine aeroplane a Group B (multi-engine aeroplanes with a maximum total weight authorised not exceeding 5,700 kg) rating is required. In practice, multi-engine aeroplanes mostly means twin-engine machines. It is not simply a matter of learning how to handle two sets of engine controls and instruments. Multi-engine aircraft are by nature more complex than single-engine machines. Most have higher performance and offer a greater variety of options regarding loading, range and take-off/landing performance than a single-engine aircraft. In particular, the handling and performance characteristics of twin-engine aircraft flying on one engine require training and practice if the advantages of two engines are to be exploited safely.

The CAA Multi-Engine Rating course has a minimum 6 hours dual flying instruction which is split into two parts, Normal Flight (2½ hours) and Asymmetric Flight (3½ hours), together with a minimum 7 hours of ground instruction followed by flight and oral tests. The flight test includes normal flight procedures applicable to the CAA PPL GFT, plus specific emergency procedures relating to multi-engine aircraft. Once issued, the privileges of Group B Rating continue to apply if the pilot has flown 5 hours as PIC in the previous 13 months (the basic currency requirement for his PPL), though only one flight need have been made in a multi-engine aircraft, and up to 2 hours of dual instruction may be included in the 5 hours total. The Group B Rating may be applied for at the same time as an initial application for a PPL, if the required instruction and test have been completed. There have been examples of student pilots completing their entire PPL courses on twin-engine aeroplanes, though few flying schools would be likely to recommend such a course, and the cost would almost certainly be prohibitive.

Under the JAA rules, expected to be introduced in July 1999, the simple multi-engine rating will no longer exist. Instead there will be four types of rating based around multi-pilot and multi-engine aircraft. For the limited scope of this book we will restrict our interest to the 'Type Rating – SPA (Single Pilot Aeroplane)' that covers multi and single engines, and the 'Class Rating Multi-Engine'.

The Type Rating – SPA allows the holder to pilot aeroplanes of the type specified in the rating. This means that the old CAA system of allowing a pilot to fly multi-engine aircraft based on a weight limit no longer exists. Each aircraft is classed and typed. 'Class' places all multi-engine piston aeroplanes in one 'division'. 'Type' separates aircraft by airworthiness certificate, handling characteristics, or minimum flight crew requirements. This is then subdivided into each type of multi-pilot aircraft; single pilot multi-engine, turboprop, turbojet; single pilot single-engine, turbojet, and any other types. The Type Rating – SPA will allow the pilot to fly only the type specified on the rating. To obtain the rating the PPL holder requires 70 hours pilot-in-command of single-engine aircraft and must have completed an approved course. The rating is valid for one year, and must be renewed in a proficiency check by flying one route sector (a take-off, departure, cruise of not less than 15 minutes, arrival, approach and landing), with an examiner. The Class rating has the same requirements to gain the rating, but is valid for two years and is renewed by a proficiency check with an authorised examiner. It appears from the JAA proposals that one approved course will qualify a pilot for both ratings, providing it is in one specific aircraft. Contact your flying training organisation or the CAA for current details.

The Instrument Rating (Aeroplanes)

Qualification for the IR requires the candidate to be a PPL holder with a night rating or a Commercial Pilot's Licence (CPL) holder. Either must have logged 50 hours cross-country flying as pilot-in-command (up to 40 hours in helicopters can count towards this) and must have passed an approved course of flight instruction. This entails 50 hours for a PPL holder, or 45 hours for a CPL holder. Twenty hours of this may be ground instrument time in a flight trainer or 35 hours in a flight simulator. Five additional hours of flight training apply if the qualification is for a multi-engine IR, and the ground time allowance also increases by 5 hours, but at least 15 hours of the total training time must be flown in a multi-engine aeroplane. Holders of a Helicopter IR may have the amount of flight training reduced to 10 hours.

An approved course of theoretical training of at least 250 hours must be completed within 18 months, and the flying training certificated by the passing of a skill test within the period of validity of the pass in theoretical examinations. The number of attempts and treatment of failures for the skill test is the same as for the PPL skill test detailed earlier in this chapter.

Instrument Rating – Aeroplanes			
Approved Course PPL(A) and night qualification or CPL(A) 50 hr cross-country experience plus approved instruction	Up to 40 hr cross-country experience may be as pilot-in-command in helicopters		
	50 hr approved instruction for single-engine IR for PPL holders or 45 hr instruction for single-engine IR for CPL holders or 50 hr instruction for multi-engine IR for CPL holders or 55 hr instruction for multi-engine IR for PPL holders	Up to 20 hr may be flight trainer or 35 hr flight simulator for multi-engine IR or 25 hr may be flight trainer or 40 hr flight simulator for multi-engine IR	For a multi-engine IR at least 15 hr of instrument flight instruction must be in multi-engine aeroplanes

The theoretical qualifications comprise air law, aircraft general knowledge, flight performance and planning, human performance and limitations, meteorology, navigation, operational procedures, and communications. The pass mark is 75%.

The Instrument Rating (Helicopters)

The CAA requirements for a helicopter IR are very similar to those for aeroplanes, but the breakdown of the hours is slightly different. Exemption from approved training is granted to PPL(A) IR holders, some qualified service personnel and pilots with more than 400 hours experience, providing the hours include certain key requirements.

<table>
<tr><th colspan="4">Instrument Rating – Helicopters – CAA requirements</th></tr>
<tr><td rowspan="4">Approved Course
PPL(H)
200 hr experience</td><td>100 hr PIC</td><td>Up to 65 hr as co-pilot acting as PIC under supervision, provided the applicant has at least 250 hr as pilot of helicopters</td><td>At least 35 hr cross-country flying</td></tr>
<tr><td rowspan="2">20 hr dual instruction in instrument flying in helicopters</td><td colspan="2">At least 5 hr must be in the type in which the applicant wishes to qualify</td></tr>
<tr><td colspan="2">The other 35 hr may be in any helicopter certified for UK instrument flight training</td></tr>
<tr><td colspan="2">20 hr instruction in instrument flying in an approved helicopter trainer or simulator</td><td>Up to 10 hr of this training may be in aeroplanes</td></tr>
</table>

Under JAA-FCL requirements due for implementation in June 2000, applicants for an IR must hold a PPL(H), a night rating and must have completed at least 50 hours cross-country flight time as PIC in helicopters or aeroplanes, of which at least 10 hours must be in helicopters. An approved training course of 50 hours instrument flying instruction must then be undertaken. Of this 50 hours, up to 15 may be instrument ground time in an approved flight and navigation trainer, or up to 25 hours in an approved flight simulator. If the rating is for a multi-engine helicopter, the total hours are increased to 55, up to 20 of which can be in a trainer or 30 hours in a simulator. At least 15 hours must be in a multi-engine helicopter. Five hours can be allowed off the total training hours if the applicant holds a CPL(H). The training culminates in a flight skill test.

The skill test is a flight test similar to that required for fixed-wing aircraft, except that in multi-engine helicopters all parts must be passed in one attempt, or the entire test has to be taken again. In the case of single-engine helicopters the candidate may fail and retake one section, but if any item is failed on the re-test

<table>
<tr><th colspan="3">Instrument Rating – Helicopters – JAA requirements</th></tr>
<tr><td rowspan="2">Single-Engine
PPL(H) plus night rating and 50 hr cross-country experience plus 50 hr instruction
or
CPL(H) plus night rating and 45 hr cross-country experience plus 50 hr instruction</td><td colspan="2">At least 10 hr in helicopters</td></tr>
<tr><td>50 hr instrument flight instruction</td><td>Up to 15 hr may be in an approved flight trainer or up to 25 hr in an approved flight simulator</td></tr>
</table>

<table>
<tr><td rowspan="3">Multi-Engine
PPL(H) plus night rating and 55 hr cross-country experience plus 50 hr instruction
or
CPL(H) plus night rating and 50 hr cross-country experience plus 50 hr instruction</td><td colspan="2">At least 15 hr in multi-engine helicopters</td></tr>
<tr><td rowspan="2">55 hr instrument flight instruction</td><td>Up to 20 hr may be in an approved flight trainer or up to 30 hr in an approved flight simulator</td></tr>
<tr><td>At least 15 hr must be in multi-engine helicopters</td></tr>
</table>

the whole test must be taken again. All parts of the skill test must be completed and passed within six months. The academic qualifications are the same as those listed above for the JAA IR for aeroplanes.

Any Questions?

To round off this chapter, here are the answers to some questions which may be in your mind.

I have done some gliding. Will it help with a PPL?

The CAA PPL rules do not permit reductions in the minimum hours flying training requirements for experienced glider pilots. However, being a current PPL(G) holder does provide an exemption from taking aviation law, flight rules and procedures, navigation and meteorology ground exams as part of the PPL(A) course. Under the JAA PPL rules, holders of pilot licences or equivalent privileges for helicopters, microlights having fixed wings and movable aerodynamic control surfaces acting in all three dimensions, gliders, self-sustaining gliders or self-launching gliders may be credited with a total of 10% of total flight time as pilot-in-command, up to a maximum of 10 hours towards a JAA PPL(A). Check with the CAA or your flying training organisation to see if any allowance is made for the academic examinations you already hold.

Are there any sponsorship schemes?

Earlier editions of this book carried details of as many as six schemes. Sadly, only two now offer financial assistance towards a PPL. The Guild of Air Pilots and Air Navigators (GAPAN, address on page 138) annually award one full PPL course with Luton

Flight Training. Applicants must be at least 17 years old, able to qualify for a CAA Class 3 medical and be available to train at Luton during the summer. In less than 100 words, applicants should send brief personal details, previous flying experience and the reason for wanting to get a PPL, to reach the Guild before the annual closing date of 16 June. The other ray of sunshine is the International Air Tattoo Flying Scholarship for disabled people. This is awarded in memory of the late Sir Douglas Bader, and partly sponsored by King Hussein of Jordan. The scheme annually provides 40 hours of flying experience on totally funded, six-week residential courses in the USA for up to nine physically handicapped applicants aged between 17–40 years. The closing date for applications is 31 December each year. Initial contact should be made to the Principal on 01285 713 300, or in writing to IAT Flying Scholarships for the Disabled, Building 15, RAF Fairford, Gloucestershire GL7 4DL.

Although it is not a direct form of flying sponsorship, many youngsters have taken jobs with flying clubs and schools under various Youth Training Schemes, and thereby learned to fly and gained their PPLs. Obviously such opportunities are limited, but they are definitely worth investigating.

I do not want to become a pilot, but I fly as a passenger and would like to learn enough to take over in an emergency.

Very wise. What you need is a Second Pilot or Safety Pilot's course (it is called a 'Pinch Hitter's' course in the USA). Most flying schools offer such training, which usually consists of 6–10 hours dual flying training and 10–20 hours ground school. This covers aircraft handling, basic navigation and use of the aircraft radio.

Although the course does not earn the student a licence or official rating, it offers two major worthwhile benefits. From the safety aspect the student should, in most circumstances, be able to land the aircraft in which he or she is travelling without injury to the aircraft or occupants. However, the more appreciated benefit will be from the additional satisfaction of knowing what is happening during the flight, removing the mystery of dials and buttons in the cockpit.

The course is a sensible 'must' for regular passengers, but be warned, many people who intend taking just the safety course catch the bug and go on to complete the entire PPL course. For an insight into basic aircraft handling and full details of the training, *The Safety Pilot's Training Manual* is available from most flying shops or direct from Airlife Publishing Ltd on 01743 235651.

Chapter 3
The Commercial Pilot

As explained in Chapter 2, the PPL is strictly an amateur qualification entitling you to fly for personal business or pleasure. The JAA defines a private pilot as 'A pilot who holds a licence which prohibits the piloting of aircraft in operations in which renumeration is given'. To receive payment for your services as a pilot, a professional qualification is a legal requirement.

Currently in force in the UK are three grades of professional flying licence: the Basic Commercial Pilot's Licence (BCPL), the Commercial Pilot's Licence (CPL), and the Air Transport Pilot's Licence (ATPL). The minimum experience requirements for these are given below, but since requirements and licence privileges can change, readers are advised to consult CAP 54, *Professional Pilot's Licences*, for the latest information on all professional licensing matters.

Basic Commercial Pilot's Licence

Barring any further changes, the BCPL will be phased out on 1 July 1999. The current requirements are a minimum age of 18 years and that the applicant holds a Class I medical certificate (or Class II for pilots with a BCPL restricted to aerial work). The approved course of training comprises a minimum of 150 hours flight training and 400 hours ground training. The flying experience requirement is at least 70 hours as PIC, of which 20 hours must be cross-country or over-sea flying, and 10 hours of instrument flying instruction. Pilots who hold a PPL(A) may also qualify for the grant of a BCPL if they have logged a minimum of 200 flying hours, of which 100 must be as PIC, of which 20 hours must be cross-country or over-sea flying, and take an abridged course of approved training consisting of 25 hours dual flying to include training for the IMC rating and BCPL GFT. If an IMC is already held, this is reduced to 15 hours training for the GFT, or

11 hours if a PPL/IR is held. Qualified UK military service pilots with 200 hours experience *may* be exempt from the approved training.

<table>
<tr><th colspan="5">Basic Commercial Pilot's Licence – Aeroplanes – CAA rating due to be phased out 1 July 1999</th></tr>
<tr><td rowspan="2">Unabridged Approved Course</td><td rowspan="2">150 hr training</td><td>70 hr PIC</td><td>20 hr cross-country or over-sea</td><td>Including a cross-country flight of at least 300 nm landing at two different aerodromes</td></tr>
<tr><td colspan="3">10 hr instrument instruction</td></tr>
<tr><td rowspan="2">Abridged Course</td><td rowspan="2">200 flying hours</td><td>100 hr PIC</td><td>20 hr cross-country or over-sea</td><td>Including a cross-country flight of at least 300 nm landing at two different aerodromes</td></tr>
<tr><td colspan="3">25 hr of approved IMC and BCPL GFT dual training or, if IMC held, 15 hr approved dual training for the GFT, or, if PPL/IR held, 11 hr approved training</td></tr>
</table>

Applicants for BCPL (Aeroplanes) must take ground examinations in aviation law, flight rules and procedures, meteorology, flight instruments and radio aids, flight planning and navigation procedures, signals, aircraft (general), aircraft (type), performance, loading, human performance and limitations, and radiotelephony. The flying training includes the requirement to pass a three-part GFT conducted by a CAA Flight Examiner in a single-engine aircraft. This comprises tests in cross-country flight, basic aircraft handling and instrument flying (GFTs 1, 2 and 3), and is identical to the GFT for the issue of a CPL, from which BCPL holders are then usually exempt. Before sitting the BCPL ground examinations, candidates must produce evidence of having completed a course of study given by an 'aeronautical study centre' (not necessarily a flying training school) recognised by the CAA. There are several of these, and the CAA can supply a list which is updated monthly. BCPL examination candidates must have logged at least 100 hours qualifying flying experience before sitting the examinations. With all professional licensing requirements there are further exemptions for specific cases which are too involved and complex to be dealt with in this book. CAP 54 – *Professional Pilots' Licences*, or the CAA's flight crew licensing department should always be consulted for specific information.

The BCPL(A) entitles the holder to fly as PIC or copilot of any aeroplane for which the licence holds a valid aircraft rating for any purpose other than public transport. If a BCPL holder has logged 400 hours as PIC, he or she may act as P1 on public transport flights in aircraft weighing less than 2,300 kg all-up weight which start and finish at the same aerodrome and do not extend beyond 25 nautical miles (pleasure flying, for example), or as copilot on public transport flights in aircraft not exceeding 5,700 kg.

Therefore, public transport exceptions aside, the BCPL covers what is known as 'aerial work', which, according to the JAA definition, are activities such as agriculture, construction, sling operations, photography, surveying, observation and patrol and aerial advertising. With appropriate ratings it also permits the holder to give flying instruction, and details of this are explained in a later chapter. BCPL holders with at least 300 hours PIC who wish to obtain an instrument or further type rating may be lucky enough to qualify for a £2,000 Hunting Aviation Flying Award. The closing date for applications is 1 August, and further enquiries should be made to Mrs K Peterson of the Guild of Air Pilots and Air Navigators. Her address and contact number appears on page 138.

CAA Commercial Pilot's Licence – Aeroplanes

The British CPL rating is technically an International Civil Aviation Authority (ICAO) VFR rating, but for the purposes of this book we will class it as a CAA rating. The minimum age under CAA and JAA rules is 18 years, and the applicant must hold a CAA Class I or JAA Class 1 medical certificate, depending upon which course is undertaken. The CAA approved course of training consists of about 600 hours of ground school. Flying experience requirements are for 155 flying hours minimum, of which 100 hours must be as PIC including 20 hours cross-country, 10 hours night flying and 10 hours of instrument flying instruction. For a combined CPL and IR (CPL/IR), there is an approved course of 200 hours minimum duration, including 150 hours as PIC, 35 hours cross-country flying, 40 hours of instrument flying and 35 hours on multi-engine aeroplanes. These minima apply to *ab initio* trainees taking recognised courses approved by the CAA. Commercial licence applicants who are already experienced pilots may be granted an exemption from taking the course, or part of it, if their total flying experience meets the CAA minimum of 700 hours.

All applicants must pass the CPL technical examinations, which consist of written papers and oral and practical tests in aviation

<table>
<tr><th colspan="4">Commercial Pilot's Licence – Aeroplanes and Combined CPL Instrument Rating – CAA rating</th></tr>
<tr><td rowspan="6">Approved Course CPL Only

155 flying hours
100 hr PIC</td><td>20 hr cross-country or over-sea flying</td><td colspan="2">Including a cross-country flight of at least 300 nautical miles, landing at two different aerodromes</td></tr>
<tr><td rowspan="4">10 hr night flying</td><td colspan="2">At least 5 hr as PIC</td></tr>
<tr><td colspan="2">At least ten take-offs and landings without assistance</td></tr>
<tr><td colspan="2">Two cross-country flights terminating at an aerodrome not less than 65 nautical miles from the point of departure</td></tr>
<tr><td>3 hr dual night instruction</td><td>At least 1 hr navigation training</td></tr>
<tr><td colspan="3">10 hr instrument flying instruction</td></tr>
<tr><td rowspan="8">Approved Course CPL/IR

200 flying hours
150 hr PIC</td><td colspan="3">At least 35 hr cross-country flying</td></tr>
<tr><td rowspan="4">10 hr night flying</td><td colspan="2">At least 5 hr as PIC</td></tr>
<tr><td colspan="2">At least 10 take-offs and landings without assistance</td></tr>
<tr><td colspan="2">Two cross-country flights terminating at an aerodrome not less than 65 nautical miles from the point of departure</td></tr>
<tr><td>3 hr dual night instruction</td><td>At least 1 hr navigation training</td></tr>
<tr><td colspan="3">10 hr instrument flying instruction</td></tr>
<tr><td>Not less than 40 hr as pilot by sole reference to instruments</td><td colspan="2">Up to 20 hr may be in an approved trainer, flight simulator or in helicopters</td></tr>
<tr><td colspan="3">At least 35 hr on multi-engine aeroplanes</td></tr>
</table>

law, flight rules and procedures, flight planning, navigation instruments, meteorology, radio aids, aircraft navigation, instruments, aircraft (general), aircraft (type), performance, loading, human performance and limitations, and radiotelephony. They are also required to take a GFT which includes demonstrations of the applicant's basic handling, cross-country, and instrument flying, conducted by a CAA Flight Examiner at one of seven regional CAA flight test centres, usually in a single-engine aeroplane. Those applying for a CPL/IR must also undergo an IR flight test on a multi-engine aircraft. Holders of BCPLs are usually exempt from certain ground examination subjects if they were passed within the previous five years, and are exempt from the CPL GFT.

JAA Commercial Pilot's Licence – Aeroplanes

As the JAA CPL licensing requirements are due for implementation on 1 July 1999, it is likely that any pilot working towards a CPL will take the JAA course rather than the CAA CPL course and later convert it to a JAA qualification. The requirements for the JAA CPL are therefore explained in detail. The minimum age for applicants is 18 years, and they must hold a Class I JAA medical certificate. There are two types of approved course. The integrated course runs for a period of 9 to 24 months and caters for training from *ab initio* right up to CPL. The theoretical training comprises of at least 400 hours instruction, but this is reduced to 350 hours for PPL holders. Flying training is 150 hours. To take the modular course the applicant needs to be a PPL holder with 200 hours experience (detailed in the table below), and this reduces the amount of flight instruction to 25 hours dual, of which 10 hours is instrument instruction. Under either system, the rating has a restriction of 50 nautical miles for the carriage of passengers until the CPL holder acquires an instrument rating or 500 hours total flying experience. Theoretical examinations are in air law, aircraft general knowledge, flight performance and planning, human performance and limitations, meteorology, navigation, operational procedures, principles of flight, and communications. The pass mark is 75%. Both courses end with a skill test which, if successful, results in the issue of the rating.

A useful extension to the CPL, and an essential one for decent employment prospects, is an instrument rating. The JAA also operates an integrated CPL/IR course that runs for the same time as the CPL course and includes the same examinations, but has an increased theoretical knowledge syllabus of 650 hours. The flying training requirements are increased beyond that of a CPL, and are detailed in the following table.

Commercial Pilot's Licence – Helicopters

So far we have been concerned with training on fixed-wing aircraft. However, the increasing importance of helicopters in commercial aviation makes a rotary-wing licence a valuable asset for a professional pilot. In 1968 there were just 136 civil helicopters registered in the UK; in 1998 there were 906.

The Commercial Pilot's Licence (Helicopters) (CPL(H)) requirements differ from those for fixed-wing pilots because there

Commercial Pilot's Licence – Aeroplanes – JAA rating and Integrated CPL/IR JAA rating		
Integrated Course CPL 150 hr flight time	10 hr may be instrument ground time	
	20 hr may be in helicopters and/or touring motorgliders	
	70 hr as PIC	
	20 hr of cross-country as PIC	Including a cross-country flight of at least 300 nautical miles, landing at two different aerodromes
	10 hr instrument instruction time	Up to 5 hr may be instrument ground time
	5 hr night flight time	
Experienced Course CPL 200 flying hours	10 hr may be instrument ground time	
	30 hr may be in helicopters, motor-gliders or gliders	Not more than 10 hr or 10% of the time flown in gliders, self-launching gliders or self-sustaining gliders may be credited
	100 hr as PIC	
	20 hr of cross-country as PIC	Including a cross-country flight of at least 300 nautical miles, landing at two different aerodromes
	10 hr instrument instruction time	Up to 5 hr may be instrument ground time
	5 hr night flight time	
Integrated Course CPL/IR 150 hr flying training	Up to 10 hr may be instrument ground time	
	70 hr PIC	20 hr instrument flight time as student pilot-in-command (SPIC)
	50 hr cross-country flight as PIC	Including a cross-country flight of at least 300 nautical miles landing at two different aerodromes
	70 hr of instrument flight instruction	Up to 10 hr may be ground time in a flight trainer or simulator
		20 hr as SPIC
	5 hr of night flying	Five solo take-offs and full-stop landings
		3 hr dual instruction
		1 hr night navigation

is no BCPL equivalent for helicopter pilots. The current CAA approved course for the CPL(H) calls for a minimum of 150 hours flight training, of which 100 hours must be on helicopters; the remainder may be on aeroplanes. The minimum hours for required sections are shown on the following table. The approved course also requires about 600 hours of ground training. For self-improvers the minimum number of flying hours to qualify for exemption from the approved course is 400 hours on helicopters. The age, medical, ground examination and flight test requirements are similar to those for fixed-wing commercial licences.

<table>
<tr><th colspan="6">Commercial Pilot's Licence – Helicopters – CAA rating</th></tr>
<tr><td rowspan="5">Approved Course
150 training hours</td><td rowspan="4">At least 100 hr in helicopters</td><td rowspan="4">35 hr as PIC</td><td rowspan="2">10 hr cross-country or over-sea flying as PIC</td><td colspan="2">Including a day flight with a landing at least 50 miles from the point of departure</td></tr>
<tr><td colspan="2">Including a night flight landing at least 50 miles from the point of departure</td></tr>
<tr><td rowspan="2">5 hr night flying as PIC or PIC under instruction</td><td>Not less than 3 hr dual instruction</td><td>Including 1 hr cross-country flying</td></tr>
<tr><td colspan="2">Five take-offs, circuits and landings</td></tr>
<tr><td colspan="5">10 hr instruction in instrument flying</td></tr>
</table>

Under the JAA-FCL provisions the requirements for a CPL-fall into three formats: by training on an approved integrated course, on a modular course, or by qualification of experience. Whichever method is chosen, the holder must be at least 18 years of age and must hold a valid JAR-FCL Class 1 medical certificate.

Candidates attending an integrated course (of between eight and 16 months) must receive a total of at least 135 hours training, including flying tests. The 135 hours must include at least 100 hours of dual instruction, of which up to 5 hours may be instrument ground time, 35 hours as PIC, 10 hours of cross-country as PIC including a flight of at least 100 nautical miles with landings at two different aerodromes, 5 hours of night flying including five solo circuits including a solo landing, and 3 hours dual instruction including 1 hour night navigation and 10 hours basic instrument flight instruction, of which up to 5 hours may be instrument ground time.

Qualification under the modular course requires the applicant to be a PPL(H) holder with a night rating and at least 155 hours of flight time including 50 hours as PIC and 10 hours cross-country. The theoretical knowledge (of around 400 hours) and flight instruction must be completed within a 12-month period. The flight instruction for applicants without an instrument rating requires at least 30 hours of dual flight instruction including 10 hours of basic instrument training, of which up to 5 hours may be instrument ground time. Applicants with a valid instrument rating require only 20 hours dual visual flight instruction, including at least 5 hours of cross-country flight.

Pilots who have not graduated via an integrated flying training course and have logged sufficient hours can take the 'experience' route. The flight time under this method is increased to 185 hours. Ten hours may be instrument ground time, and 20 hours of the 185 hours may have been flown in aeroplanes, motorgliders or gliders. Of this 20 hours, not more than 10 hours or 10% (whichever is the least) of the time flown on gliders may be taken into account. Fifteen hours of this may have been flown in aeroplanes and/or touring motorgliders, and up to 10 hours may be claimed for instrument ground time. All applicants must have 50 hours as PIC (or 35 hours if completed during an integrated flying training course) and 10 hours of cross-country flight time, including a cross-country flight of at least 100 nautical miles within which two full-stop landings at different aerodromes must be made. They are also required to have logged 10 hours of instrument instruction time (including up to 5 hours of instrument ground time) and 5 hours night flight time.

All routes to the CPL(H) culminate in a flying skill test. All applicants for a CPL(H) must have completed a course of instruction at an approved flying training organisation or at an organisation specialising in theoretical knowledge instruction. The written examinations comprise air law, aircraft general knowledge, flight performance and planning, human performance and limitations, meteorology, navigation and operational procedures and communications. A 75% pass mark is required for each subject, and a partial pass will be awarded to applicants achieving a pass in at least 50% of the examination as a whole. Two re-sits of the failed papers are allowed, but a failure to have passed all on the third attempt will result in the whole set of examinations being re-sat, after further compulsory training *as determined by the competent authority*. The complete set of examinations must be passed within a 12-month period, and a pass will be accepted for the grant of the CPL(H) during the 36 months from the date of first gaining a pass or partial pass.

CAA Commercial helicopter pilot training approved courses are offered by three operators, Cabair, Bristow and Oxford Air Training School (see listing on page 134), but at the time of writing sponsorship is non-existent. Of those companies which have had sponsored training in the past, perhaps the best known is Bristow Helicopters at Redhill, Surrey, whose own training school has been operating for more than 30 years and, until 1993, trained some 30

<table>
<tr><th colspan="6">Commercial Pilot's Licence – Helicopters – JAA rating</th></tr>
<tr><td rowspan="4">Integrated Course
135 hr flying training</td><td rowspan="2">100 hr dual instruction</td><td rowspan="4">(a) 15 hr may be in aeroplanes and/or touring motor gliders
(b) Up to 10 hr may be instrument ground time</td><td>10 hr basic instrument flight instruction</td><td colspan="2">5 hr may be ground instrument time</td></tr>
<tr><td rowspan="2">5 hr night flying</td><td>3 hr dual instruction</td><td>1 hr night navigation instruction</td></tr>
<tr><td rowspan="2">35 hr PIC in helicopters</td><td colspan="2">Five solo circuits and landings</td></tr>
<tr><td colspan="3">10 hr cross-country, including a cross-country flight totalling at least 100 nautical miles in the course of which two landings at two different aerodromes is made</td></tr>
<tr><td rowspan="3">Modular Course
PPL(H) plus 155 hr flight time and a night rating</td><td colspan="5">50 hr PIC</td></tr>
<tr><td colspan="5">10 hr cross-country</td></tr>
<tr><td colspan="2">Dual flight instruction</td><td colspan="3">If no IR – 30 hr including 10 hr basic instrument training (up to 5 hr can be ground instrument time). If an IR held – 20 hr visual flight instruction including at least 5 hr cross-country</td></tr>
<tr><td rowspan="5">Experienced Route
185 hr flight time</td><td colspan="5">50 hr PIC (or 35 hr if completed during an integrated course)</td></tr>
<tr><td colspan="5">10 hr cross-country</td></tr>
<tr><td colspan="5">10 hr may be instrument ground time</td></tr>
<tr><td colspan="3">5 hr night flying</td><td colspan="2"></td></tr>
<tr><td colspan="3">Up to 20 hr may be in aeroplanes, motorgliders and gliders (a minimum of 10 hr must be aeroplanes or motorgliders if this allowance is claimed)</td><td colspan="2">No more than 10 hr or 10% of glider time (whichever less) is claimable</td></tr>
</table>

students each year, mostly to fill first-officer positions in its own fleet.

Because there is no BCPL and no provisions for gaining experience and earning money through flying instruction with a full CPL, the self-improver option is not really viable for helicopter pilots. Operating costs, and therefore the costs of hiring helicopters, are much higher than for aeroplanes, making hours-building towards the (current CAA minimum) 400 hours an expensive business, probably much more expensive than paying for an approved CPL(H) in the first place.

For anyone thinking of a career in civil helicopter flying, an enquiry to the British Helicopter Advisory Board (see page 138) would probably be as good a starting point as any, and first gaining a PPL(H) would improve one's admittedly limited chances of sponsorship to a commercial licence.

Air Transport Pilot's Licence – Aeroplanes

This is the ultimate rating that can be added to a PPL. Under CAA and JAA rules, the minimum age is 21 years and candidates must hold a Class I medical certificate and must have logged 1,500 hours of flight experience. Under the CAA rules this experience must be made up as follows:

1. Not less than 250 hours must be as PIC of an aeroplane; 150 of those hours may be as copilot acting as PIC U/S.
2. 50 hours cross-country or over-sea flying as PIC or PIC U/S of aeroplanes or helicopters, 35 hours of which must be in aeroplanes, including a route of at least 300 nautical miles with landings at two different aerodromes.
3. A further 150 hours cross-country or over-sea flying as PIC or PIC U/S. Copilot time under this section may be counted as half-time, that is two hours flown as copilot will count as one hour under this requirement. Of these hours, 65 hours must be in aeroplanes.
4. 100 hours night flying as PIC, PIC U/S or copilot. Up to half of this time may be in helicopters, and at least 25 hours must be on cross-country or over-sea flights as PIC or PIC U/S, including two flights terminating at an aerodrome not less than 65 nautical miles from the point of departure. The night flying time must include at least 5 hours, ten take-offs and ten landings as PIC. Exemptions are granted in respect of the cross-country requirements for CPL(H) and ATPL(H) holders.

5 75 hours flying as pilot by sole reference to instruments, of which at least 50 hours must be in aeroplanes. The remainder may be in an aeroplane, a helicopter or an approved simulator.

<table>
<tr><th colspan="4">Airline Transport Pilot's Licence – Aeroplanes – CAA rating</th></tr>
<tr><td rowspan="9">ATPL
1,500 flying hours</td><td>250 hr PIC</td><td colspan="2">Up to 150 hr as copilot acting as PIC U/S</td></tr>
<tr><td>50 hr cross-country or over-sea as PIC or PIC U/S</td><td>At least 35 hr must be PIC in aeroplanes</td><td>Including a route of at least 300 nautical miles with landings at two different aerodromes</td></tr>
<tr><td rowspan="2">A further 150 hr cross-country or over-sea as PIC or PIC U/S</td><td colspan="2">65 of these hours must be in aeroplanes</td></tr>
<tr><td colspan="2">Copilot time can count, but only as half time</td></tr>
<tr><td rowspan="3">100 hr night flying as PIC, PIC U/S or copilot</td><td colspan="2">Up to 50 hr may be in helicopters</td></tr>
<tr><td>25 hr must be cross-country or over-sea</td><td>Including two flights terminating at an aerodrome not less than 65 nautical miles from the point of departure</td></tr>
<tr><td colspan="2">5 hr, ten take-offs and ten landings must be as PIC</td></tr>
<tr><td rowspan="2">75 hr instrument flying</td><td colspan="2">50 hr must be in aeroplanes</td></tr>
<tr><td colspan="2">25 hr may be in aeroplanes, helicopters or approved simulators</td></tr>
</table>

5 The balance of hours may be made up of:

a Any PIC time, counted in full.

b Any pilot under instruction time, counted in full.

c PIC U/S time, counted in full up to 550 hours, or as half time for any hours in excess of 550 hours.

d As copilot, counted at half-time. Time as a PPL holder is limited to 100 hours (counted as 50 hours).

Further allowances are made for time as a Systems Panel Operator or Flight Engineer, one hour being allowed for three flown, up to a maximum of 900 hours with 300 claimable. Time in microlight and self-launching motorgliders may also be claimed towards the total hours required up to a maximum of 100 hours, but not towards the individual flight requirements. Under this allowance the self-launching motorglider time can only be counted while the aircraft is under power. For full and current details refer to CAP 54.

Commercial Licence holders upgrading to ATPL are not usually required to take another flight test. Those, in broad terms, are the licensing requirements for UK professional pilots' licences. Thus, three principle routes are available to becoming a

Robinson R22 is the most widely-used light helicopter for civilian rotary wing training in Britain, where more than 250 are operating. (Sloane Helicopters)

Simple uncluttered instrument console of the Robinson R22. (Sloane Helicopters)

Aircraft of the British Aerospace Flying College fleet at Prestwick Airport. Top to bottom: Piper Seneca III, Warrior II and FFA Wren. (British Aerospace)

Simulators are a vital part of the airline pilot training and are incredibly realistic. This is British Airways' latest Boeing 747-400 simulator on final approach at the end of a night 'flight'. (Rediffusion Simulation)

The Beech Duchess is typical of light twin-engined aircraft used for multi-engine PPL and CPL training. This one is part of the large training fleet of Wycombe Air Centre in Buckinghamshire. (WAC)

professional pilot. The direct route via a purpose-designed BCPL, CPL or CPL/IR course, bypassing the PPL entirely; or the 'self-improvement' route whereby a private pilot can build up the required minimum of 200 or 700 hours towards a BCPL or CPL. Barring any futher changes, the BCPL be phased out on 1 July 1999.

Under the JAA rules, the total hours requirement for the experienced route is the same, 1,500 hours, and the minimum rating requirement is a PPL, but existing CPL holders get a 350 hours reduction in the required hours, and IR holders 250 hours. The breakdown of requirements is slightly different. In addition there is an integrated course which provides for training from *ab initio* level and includes training to, and the issue of, a CPL(A), a multi-engine instrument rating and instruction in multi-crew co-operation. It is aimed at training pilots to a level of proficiency to enable them to operate as copilot on multi-pilot, multi-engine aircraft in commercial air transportation. For existing PPL(A) holders, 50% of the hours flown by the entrant before the course may be credited towards the course flight time, up to a maximum of 40 hours experience. Of those, 20 hours can be dual instruction. The following table gives details of the breakdown of training for both routes. All of the required hours must be completed before the ATPL skill test may be taken.

In the integrated course, all theoretical training must be completed within the same continuous approved course lasting between 12 and 30 months and comprising at least 1,000 hours of instruction. The subjects are broken down as follows, with the minimum number of instructional hours for each shown in brackets: air law (90), aircraft general knowledge (110), flight performance and planning (140), human performance and limitations (70), meteorology (100), navigation (270), operational procedures (20), principles of flight (50), and communications (60). Applicants taking the experienced route also require the academic qualifications, and they must be attained by taking a modular Air Transport Pilot Theory Course. Partial exemptions may be possible for CPL(A) and IR holders.

Helicopters

The CAA ATPL for helicopters calls for 1,200 hours experience of flying machines, of which 400 hours must be as PIC of helicopters or made up as shown in the table below. To make up the required

<table>
<tr><th colspan="5">Airline Transport Pilot's Licence – Aeroplanes – JAA rating</th></tr>
<tr><td rowspan="6">ATPL
Experienced course

1,500 hr of flight time</td><td>250 hr PIC</td><td colspan="3">Up to 150 hr as copilot performing as PIC</td></tr>
<tr><td colspan="4">500 hr in multi-pilot operations</td></tr>
<tr><td colspan="4">Up to 100 hr may be in a flight simulator</td></tr>
<tr><td>200 hr cross-country</td><td colspan="3">At least 100 hr must be a PIC</td></tr>
<tr><td colspan="4">100 hr night flying</td></tr>
<tr><td colspan="4">75 hr instrument flight time</td></tr>
<tr><td rowspan="11">ATPL – co-pilot
Approved Integrated Course

Provides qualification of a CPL(A) with instrument rating and to copilot on multi-pilot, multi-engine aeroplanes in commercial air transportation</td><td rowspan="11">195 hr flying training (hours can form a combined function)</td><td colspan="3">Up to 55 hr instrument ground time</td></tr>
<tr><td colspan="2" rowspan="2">100 hr PIC</td><td>50 hr VFR flight</td></tr>
<tr><td>50 hr instrument flight as SPIC</td></tr>
<tr><td colspan="2">50 hr cross-country as PIC</td><td>Including a cross-country flight of at least 300 nautical miles, landing at two different aerodromes</td></tr>
<tr><td colspan="2" rowspan="3">5 hr night flight</td><td>Five solo take-offs and full-stop landings</td></tr>
<tr><td>3 hr dual instruction</td></tr>
<tr><td>1 hr night navigation</td></tr>
<tr><td rowspan="4">115 hr of instrument flight time</td><td rowspan="2">50 hr instrument flight instruction</td><td>Up to 25 hr instrument ground time in a flight trainer</td></tr>
<tr><td>Up to 40 hr in an approved flight simulator</td></tr>
<tr><td colspan="2">50 hr as student PIC</td></tr>
<tr><td>15 hr multi-crew co-operation</td><td>May all be simulator time</td></tr>
</table>

hours, 100 hours can be flown in microlights and, providing the other minimum flying requirements are complied with, there is no limit to the number of hours claimed on self-launching motorgliders (provided the aircraft is under power) or normal fixed-wing aircraft, subject to the following: PIC and pilot-under-instruction time can be counted in full; PIC U/S time can be counted to a maximum of 365 hours, any PIC U/S time more than this counting only at half rate; copilot time counts at half rate, and copilot experience gained as the holder of a PPL can count but is limited to 100 hours and only counts as 50 hours, at half rate. The ground examinations are the same as for the CAA CPL(H).

<table>
<tr><th colspan="5">Airline Transport Pilot's Licence – Helicopters – CAA rating</th></tr>
<tr><td rowspan="9">ATPL

1,200 hr as pilot of flying machines</td><td colspan="4">400 hr PIC of helicopters or 50 hr PIC of flying machines, 35 hr of which must be in helicopter plus 165 hr as PIC or as copilot acting as PIC under supervision (U/S) of helicopters, plus 200 hr PIC in helicopters (or as copilot in helicopters counted at half rate)</td></tr>
<tr><td colspan="2" rowspan="2">10 hr cross-country or over-sea flying as PIC in helicopters</td><td colspan="2">Including at least 1 day flight with a landing at least 50 miles from the point of departure</td></tr>
<tr><td colspan="2">Including at least 1 night flight with a landing at least 50 miles from the point of departure</td></tr>
<tr><td colspan="2">A further 40 hr cross-country or over-sea flying as PIC or PIC U/S in helicopters or aeroplanes</td><td colspan="2">At least 15 hr must be in helicopters</td></tr>
<tr><td rowspan="4">20 hr night flying in helicopters as PIC, PIC U/S or pilot-under-instruction</td><td colspan="2">At least 3 hr dual instruction</td><td>1 hr cross-country flying</td></tr>
<tr><td colspan="3">5 hr as PIC</td></tr>
<tr><td colspan="3">A further 5 hr as PIC or PIC U/S</td></tr>
<tr><td colspan="3">At least five take-offs, circuits and landings without assistance</td></tr>
<tr><td colspan="4">10 hr instruction in instrument flying in helicopters</td></tr>
</table>

The JAA-FCL requirements for an ATPL (Helicopters) fall into two formats: either by training with an approved in integrated course or by qualification of experience. Either way, the holder must be at least 21 years of age and must hold a valid JAR-FCL Class 1 medical certificate. For the experienced route they must already hold a CPL(H), a multi-engine rating and a helicopter instrument rating.

The integrated course can start at *ab initio* level, and provides the qualification of a CPL(H) with instrument rating. It is aimed at training pilots to a level of proficiency to enable them to operate as copilot on multi-pilot, multi-engine helicopters in commercial air transportation. The course comprises theoretical instruction of around 800 hours, visual and instrument flying training and multi-crew/multi-pilot helicopter training, and can last between one and two years. The flying training comprises at least:

1. Flying training of at least 195 hours, of which 35 hours may be instrument ground time.
2. 95 hours of dual instruction, of which not more than 35 hours may be instrument ground time.
3. 100 hours as PIC, including 34 hours visual flight rules (VFR) flight, plus 1 hour night flight and 65 hours as student pilot-in-command.
4. 5 hours of night flight, including five solo circuits and at least 3 hours dual instruction to include 1 hour night navigation.
5. 65 hours instrument flying, including:
   - **a** 35 hours of instrument flight instruction, of which no more than 10 hours may be instrument ground time in a flight trainer or 20 hours in a flight simulator.
   - **b** 15 hours as SPIC.
   - **c** 15 hours multi-crew operation, for which a flight simulator may be used.

PPL(H) holders may be credited with 50% of the hours flown before starting the course up to a maximum of 40 hours, of which no more than 20 hours may be dual instruction.

Qualification by experience, when combined with the required examination and knowledge requirements (unless exempt), results in a full ATPL. The applicant requires at least 1,000 hours of flight time, including at least:

1. 350 hours in multi-pilot operations.
2. 250 hours as PIC, or at least 100 hours as PIC and 150 hours as copilot.
3. 200 hours of cross-country flight time, of which at least 100 hours must be as PIC or copilot under supervision.
4. 70 hours of instrument time, of which no more than 30 hours may be instrument ground time.
5. 100 hours of night flying as PIC or copilot.

Holders of a pilot's licence or equivalent document for other categories of aircraft will be credited with flight time, except flight time in aeroplanes, which may only be credited as up to 50% of the total flight time requirements. The flying training concludes with a flying skill test.

<table>
<tr><th colspan="4">Airline Transport Pilot's Licence – Helicopters – JAA rating</th></tr>
<tr><td rowspan="11">ATPL – copilot Approved Integrated Course
Provides qualification of a CPL(H) with instrument rating and to copilot on multi-pilot, multi-engine helicopters in commercial air transportation

195 hr flight training</td><td rowspan="11">95 hr dual instruction and 100 hr SPIC (sub-section hours can form a combined function)

A maximum of 35 hr may be instrument ground time</td><td rowspan="3">65 hr instrument flying</td><td>35 hr instrument flight instruction</td></tr>
<tr><td>15 hr SPIC</td></tr>
<tr><td>15 hr multi-crew operation for which a simulator may be used</td></tr>
<tr><td rowspan="3">5 hr night flying</td><td>Five solo circuits</td></tr>
<tr><td>3 hr dual instruction</td></tr>
<tr><td>1 hr night navigation</td></tr>
<tr><td colspan="2">65 hr SPIC</td></tr>
<tr><td colspan="2">34 hr VFR flight as PIC</td></tr>
<tr><td colspan="2">1 hr night flight as PIC</td></tr>
<tr><td rowspan="2">50 hr cross-country as PIC</td><td>Including a flight of at least 100 nautical miles that visits and lands at two different aerodromes</td></tr>
<tr><td>At least 10 hr as SPIC</td></tr>
<tr><td rowspan="5">ATPL Qualification by Experience

1,000 hr of flight time, hold a CPL(H), a multi-engine instrument rating and received instruction in multi-crew co-operation</td><td colspan="3">350 hr multi-pilot operations</td></tr>
<tr><td>250 hr as PIC</td><td colspan="2">or 100 hr as PIC and 150 hr as copilot</td></tr>
<tr><td>200 hr cross-country</td><td colspan="2">At least 100 hr as PIC or copilot under supervision</td></tr>
<tr><td>70 hr instrument flight time</td><td colspan="2">No more than 30 hr instrument ground time</td></tr>
<tr><td colspan="3">100 hr night flying as PIC or as copilot</td></tr>
</table>

The theoretical knowledge training is tested in 14 papers, for which about 20 hours is allowed. The full examination is made up as follows:

Paper		
1	Air Law	
2	Aircraft general knowledge	– airframe/systems/powerplant
3	Instruments/electronics	
4	Flight performance and planning	– mass and balance
5		– performance
6		– flight planning and monitoring
7	Human performance and limitations	
8	Meteorology	
9	Navigation	– general navigation
10		– radio navigation
11	Operational procedures	
12	Principles of flight	
13	Communications	– VFR
14		– IFR

A 75% pass mark is required for each subject, and a partial pass will be awarded to applicants achieving a pass in at least 50% of the examination as a whole. Two re-sits of the failed papers are allowed, but a failure to pass all on the third attempt will result in the whole set of examinations being re-sat after further compulsory training as determined by the competent authority.

Commercial Pilot Licence Courses

First, there is the most direct route – an approved course leading to the issue of a CPL/IR. Several approved flying schools in the UK are offering CPL/IR courses on fixed-wing aircraft. In August 1998 the CAA listed, the British Aerospace Flying Training (UK) Ltd at Prestwick Airport, the Cabair College of Air Training at Cranfield Aerodrome and the Oxford Air Training School at Oxford Airport. These lists are updated monthly, as required.

Ab initio CPL/IR courses last about 13 months, and include full ground school, 40 hours of simulator training and a minimum of 200 hours flying on single and twin-engine light aircraft. The courses are full-time and (usually) residential. Schools usually demand minimum educational standards of five passes at GCSE Ordinary Level (or regional or national equivalent), to include English, mathematics and a science subject, preferably physics. These are school requirements and not official CAA policy, which lays down no educational standards, though most knowledgeable observers of professional pilot training say that *ab initio* students seeking professional licences should have Advanced Level GCSE passes in mathematics and physics, or they will find the CPL ground school hard-going.

It is wise, though not essential, to ensure that you meet the more stringent medical requirements for a Class I Medical Certificate before embarking on a professional licence course. Although a Class III (PPL) medical certificate is adequate for the training period, a Class I certificate must be held before a CPL can be issued, and it is obviously pointless to pursue a training course, only to find at the end of it that you are debarred from obtaining your licence for medical reasons. The first medical examination for a professional licence must be conducted by the CAA Medical Branch's own examiners. Thereafter it can be renewed by authorised medical examiners. The medical standards are higher than those for private pilots. For example, impaired hearing, while not necessarily preventing a PPL applicant from obtaining a medical certificate, would probably prohibit the issue of a professional certificate. Renewal intervals for Class I medical certificates are: CPL holders annually up to 40 years of age and six-monthly thereafter; ATPL holders must renew every six months.

How much does a CPL/IR course cost? In mid-1998 prices a full CPL/IR course would cost approximately £50,000, inclusive of ground school, flying, accommodation and VAT. Medical expenses, CAA examination and licence fees and any additional flying training needed beyond the minimum 200 hours requirement would add to that figure.

Not surprisingly, most of the self-financed students at commercial flying schools come from abroad. The alternative to paying your own way (and incidentally having the money to pay does *not* guarantee a place on a CPL/IR course unless the educational and aptitude requirements are also met), is to find a sponsor. In practice this means an airline, and the question of cadet sponsorships is dealt with in Chapter 4.

A visit to a typical commercial pilot training establishment reveals just what the CPL/IR course entails. The Oxford Air Training School, appropriately located within sight of the spires of the City of Oxford, that traditional seat of learning and scholarship, is one of the world's largest professional flight training establishments. Many of its students come from abroad, notably from the Middle East and Africa. For such students their CPL/IR training begins with a 16-week foundation course, during which they improve their use of English, especially as related to the technicalities of aviation, and adjust to the foreign environment and living away from home, often for the first time in their lives. The CPL/IR course proper lasts 52 weeks, with two more weeks set aside for vacations, and begins with an initial six-week period of intensive ground instruction. At the end of this ground school period, students take a pre-flight test before proceeding to the next stage. Most pass, the failure rate at this point being only one in a hundred. After that hurdle, the student's working week, from Monday to Friday, falls into a routine of integrated flying/ground school; one day in the classroom, one in the cockpit. No part of each 0900hr–1730hr working day is wasted, nor unnecessarily duplicated, for the 52 weeks allocated for the course is little enough. *Ab initio* flying is conducted on Piper Warrior aircraft, while advanced work for the IR, the final 35 hours of each course, is done on twin-engine Piper Senecas.

Cadets at Oxford live in comfortable motel-style study/bedrooms on the airfield. Unlike university undergraduates they are required to wear the school's blazer-and-slacks uniform during working hours, but otherwise the atmosphere is the comradely, cosmopolitan one of any university, though with longer working hours and perhaps a more purposeful air to the students, who are united by one common aim – to fly professionally, in both senses of the word. Nonetheless, there is a drop-out rate of around 25% among CPL/IR trainees. It sounds wasteful and disappointing for students to work so hard and fail to obtain their licences, but most of the failures occur very early in the course, usually within the first three months and before the students make their first solo flights. This is because the CPL/IR course is intensive from the outset, and failure to cope either in the classroom or in the air quickly manifests itself. The two elements of the course are interdependent; it is no use performing well in the air if ground study lags behind, or vice versa. One must inevitably affect the other, and since the time allocated for the course is not too generous, there is seldom an opportunity for a student who falls seriously behind to catch up.

Students take the CAA's CPL examinations in the 41st week of their course, but before that they will have taken three internal tests at the school to assess their progress: An Initial Test in week 13, an Interim Test in week 26, and the Final Test, which determines their suitability for entry for the CPL examinations, in week 39. Every three months, students' progress is monitored by a review board comprising the school principal, the CFI, the manager of ground training and the head of simulated flight, who discuss matters with each student informally before preparing a progress report, a copy of which is sent to his sponsor. Following the CPL examinations, students progress to twin-engine aircraft for the IR phase of their training. Simulators are playing an increasingly important part in professional flight training, particularly for instrument flight procedures. They save time and money, and, if used as an integral part of a well-planned training syllabus, permit more effective and economic use of aeroplanes for those parts of the syllabus which can best be taught in the air, such as take-offs and landings, recovery from unusual attitudes or visual cross-country flight. For instrument procedures, modern simulators can reproduce virtually everything that might be experienced in a real aeroplane. Indeed, when converting pilots to new aircraft types in airline service, it is now by no means unusual for a trainee to get his or her first 'feel' of the real aeroplane in the air quite late in the conversion course.

Training Concessions for Experienced Pilots

The CAA grants certain exemptions from the training requirements for Service pilots and for licensed private pilots taking the approved CPL and CPL/IR courses. Pilots qualified and serving with Her Majesty's Forces, and who are in current military flying practice with total hours exceeding the minimum licence requirements for the CPL, can count their military flight time towards a professional licence. The approved professional flying schools offer ground and flying courses specially tailored for ex-Service personnel trying to gain civilian commercial licences. Private pilots who have logged 50 hours or over may be granted a partial exemption from the minimum number of training hours laid down for approved CPL and CPL/IR courses at the discretion of the CAA. However, because of the integrated nature of CPL courses, combining alternating ground and flight elements, such exemptions will probably not reduce the total duration of the course, though they can reduce the overall cost by the number of flying hours credited for PPL experience.

Self-improvement

For those would-be commercial pilots who have no sponsors and cannot afford to pay for an approved course of instruction leading to a CPL or CPL/IR, the so-called 'self-improvement' route is a practical but not easy option.

The key to the self-improvement route lies in finding a way to build flying hours cheaply, free of charge, or, best of all, to be paid for flying, and the most common source of such flying is in training itself. In the past, flying instruction could be given by a PPL who had gained an instructor's rating, and was the usual 'ladder' by which the required 700 flying hours needed for exemption from an unabridged CPL course was reached. However, receiving payment for instruction is no longer legal for PPL-holding instructors. For that, the minimum requirement is for an AFI or FI rating and at least a Restricted BCPL, although these ratings are to change in July 1999. The current experience and training requirements for instructor ratings follow.

Assistant Flying Instructor

This rating is not recognised under the JAA regulations, and is due to be phased out in July 1999. As that date approaches, courses will be available to convert the AFI rating into the full JAA FI rating, and in any event there will be transition period of two years to allow for all rating holders to convert. To start an approved course of training for the AFI rating, those not already holding professional flying licences – i.e. candidates for a BCPL(A) – must have:

1. logged a minimum of 165 hours total flying experience in aeroplanes, of which not less than 95 hours must have been as PIC;
2. passed the GFT;
3. passed the ground examinations for the BCPL(A);
4. passed the IMC rating flight test in the preceding 25 months, or the IR flight test in the preceding 13 months; and
5. a CAA Class I or Class II medical certificate.

Those already holding a professional licence must have:

1. logged not less than 100 hours as PIC of aeroplanes, of which not less than 30 hours must be in single-engine piston-powered types;
2. not less than 35 hours as pilot-under-instruction;
3. taken a pre-entry test if less than 5 hours experience as PIC of

single-engine, piston-powered aircraft has been recorded in the preceding 13 months; and

4 a CAA Class I or Class II medical certificate.

The approved course for the AFI rating comprises not less than 55 hours ground training and 28 hours flight training, followed by a flight test and an oral ground examination by a Flying Instructor Examiner. The basic AFI rating qualifies the AFI to give instruction on single-engine aeroplanes up to PPL standard, but not to instruct in applied instrument flying, aerobatics or night flying until additional flight and ground training has been obtained and practical instructional experience has been gained which enables the restriction to be lifted. AFIs may not authorise first solo flights or first solo cross-countries, and may only instruct under the supervision of a fully qualified flying instructor.

An AFI rating also exists for helicopters but, as no BCPL is available for helicopter pilots, the qualifying requirements are different. Before being permitted to enter an approved training course, the applicant must have flown at least 300 hours as PIC in helicopters, including at least 15 hours immediately preceding the start of the course. A general handling flight test must also be passed before the flight test can be taken, and the applicant must have flown at least 30 hours as PIC on the type of helicopter to be endorsed on the rating and in which the test is to be taken. Fifteen of these hours must have been flown in the six months preceding the test.

The minimum approved course training is 50 hours ground and 25 hours flight training. As with the aeroplane rating, the applicant cannot conduct training in applied instrument or night flying until additional flight and ground training experience has been obtained and practical instructional experience has been gained which enables the restriction to be lifted.

Flying Instructor

To apply for a CAA Flying Instructor rating, applicants must have logged a minimum 400 hours as PIC of aeroplanes, including not less than 200 instructional hours (or they must have been an AFI or QFI in the UK military forces for not less than six months). A flight test and oral ground examination must also be passed.

Ground studies for the required BCPL can take the form of a correspondence course or an intensive (usually residential) course at one of the CAA-approved ‘aeronautical study centres’. Rather than sitting the basic BCPL ground examinations, it makes sense to opt instead for the CPL examinations. These results can be 'banked' for a period of up to five years while the necessary hours needed for the issue of the licence are accumulated. Even those PPLs who can meet the minimum experience requirements for the issue of a BCPL will also require some flight training to prepare for GFTs 1, 2 and 3. Flying training for the BCPL GFTs is more expensive than for the PPL. Allowing for, say, a minimum of 20 hours instruction at an average of £150 per hour, the cost of exam study courses and CAA flight test and exam fees, a 'self-improver' BCPL is probably going to cost about £4,500, and an AFI course another £3,500–£4,500. One training specialist who has analysed costings estimates the real cost of a BCPL with AFI rating at more than £20,000 by factoring in the cost of getting a PPL, hours-building before applying for the professional licence, and the likelihood of having to retake part of the ground examinations and flight tests, with accompanying fees each time.

For the helicopter FI rating, applicants must have logged 500 hours experience as PIC with not less than 200 hours as an instructor on helicopters. The PIC time must include at least 30 hours on the type of helicopter to be endorsed on the rating. As there is no BCPL for helicopters, the applicant must take the CPL route. From a cost point of view, a full CPL and FI rating is best reserved for helicopter-mad National Lottery winners, unless exemption from training is gained from UK military forces training.

The hours required for the JAA Flight Instructor's rating are seemingly lower, as only 200 hours of flight time is required. This must include 30 hours of single piston-engine time, 10 hours of instrument flight instruction and 20 hours of cross-country flying. However, passing the course at this level would only result in a restricted FI rating. For the restriction to be removed, the restricted FI needs to have completed at least 100 hours of flight instruction, to have supervised at least 25 student solo flights, and to receive a recommendation for an unrestricted FI rating from a supervising FI. On completion of 500 hours total flying time, the options are then available via various approved courses to extend the rating to instruct CPL, single pilot multi and class ratings and PPL flying instructor students. For each rating the instructor needs to hold the rating being instructed. For instance, a CPL instructor needs to hold a CPL, 500 hours and an FI rating. However, even before beginning an approved FI course to attain a basic FI rating, the applicant must have the knowledge and exam requirements for a CPL(A), must have flown the required hours and must pass a pre-entry flight test. In the long term, with five years' flight instruction under your belt and 200 hours instrument flying, the qualification can be extended to instruct pilots to IR standard. The ratings do not end there, after all, someone has to instruct multi-engine, multi-pilot instructors, but as that requires 1,500 hours on multi-pilot aircraft and a few other requisites, this book will restrict itself to the PPL instructor's rating requirements.

<table>
<tr><th colspan="4">Flying Instructor – Aeroplanes – JAA rating (to instruct to PPL student level)</th></tr>
<tr><td rowspan="7">Instructor

200 flying hours</td><td colspan="3">100 hr as PIC if holding an ATPL(A)
or 150 hr as PIC if holding a PPL(A)</td></tr>
<tr><td>At least 30 hr in single-engine piston aircraft</td><td colspan="2">5 hr must have been completed during the six months preceding the pre-entry flight test</td></tr>
<tr><td>10 hr instrument flight instruction</td><td colspan="2">Not more than 5 hr in a flight trainer or simulator</td></tr>
<tr><td>20 hr cross-country as PIC</td><td colspan="2">Including a cross-country flight of at least 300 nautical miles, landing at two different aerodromes</td></tr>
<tr><td rowspan="2">30 hr flight instruction</td><td>25 hr must be dual flight instruction</td><td>5 hr may be mutual flying (with another applicant)</td></tr>
<tr><td colspan="2">5 hr may be in an approved flight trainer or simulator</td></tr>
<tr><td colspan="3">The skill test is additional to the training time</td></tr>
</table>

Helicopters

With the qualification requirements for instructor ratings set to change in June 2000, it seems most logical to list only the JAA-FCL requirements for helicopter instructor ratings. Details of the requirements currently in force can be obtained from any helicopter training school qualified to provide instructor training, but by June 2000 the rating requirements will be as follows:

The minimum age for an unrestricted FI Helicopters rating is 18 years. Before candidates can start training they must have completed at least 300 hours of flight time, of which 100 hours must be as PIC if holding an ATPL(H) or CPL(H), or 200 hours as PIC if holding a PPL(H). Ten hours of instrument flight instruction must have been received, of which 5 hours may be instrument ground time in a flight simulator or trainer. At least 20 hours of cross-country flight as PIC must have been logged, including a flight of not less than 100 nautical miles within which two full-stop landings at two different aerodromes must have been made. A specific pre-entry flight test is also required to be passed within the six months preceding the start of the training course, and an approved course of theoretical knowledge instruction must also have been passed. The flight training comprises at least 30 hours of instruction, including 25 hours dual. The remaining 5 hours can be mutual flying (two trainees flying together). The rating, when issued, is initially on a restricted basis and only allows instruction for PPL(H) and night ratings. This restriction is lifted after the instructor has completed at least 100 hours of flight instruction, supervised 25 student solo flights and received a recommendation from a supervising instructor. Although then classed as unrestricted, the rating does not allow the instructor to carry out all types of flight instruction until at least 500 hours of flight time in helicopters has been logged.

<table>
<tr><th colspan="3">Instrument Rating – Helicopters – JAA requirements</th></tr>
<tr><td rowspan="5">Minimum 300 hr flight time plus 30 hr flight training</td><td colspan="2">200 hr PIC if a PPL(H) holder or
100 hr PIC if a ATPL(H) or CPL(H) holder</td></tr>
<tr><td>10 hr instrument instruction</td><td>5 hr may be instrument ground time</td></tr>
<tr><td>20 hr cross-country as PIC</td><td>Including a flight of at least 100 nautical miles that visits and lands at two different aerodromes</td></tr>
<tr><td rowspan="2">30 hr FI flight training</td><td>25 hr dual instruction</td></tr>
<tr><td>5 hr may be 'mutual flying'</td></tr>
</table>

Some large flying schools offer sponsorship schemes whereby selected PPLs have some or all their AFI course fees paid in return for a period of instructing on the staff of the school. The Cabair Group based at Cranfield Aerodrome and Oxford Air Training School's General Aviation Centre are among those which have in the past provided such sponsorship training, and can point to many former AFIs who have gone on to gain a CPL and ATPL thanks to this initial 'leg-up'.

Another possible source of finance for BCPL or AFI courses is the government-sponsored Career Development Loan Scheme, which provides loans of between £200–£5,000 to cover up to 80% of the cost of a vocational training course. Details are available from any Job Centre, or from Freepost Career Development, PO Box 99, Sudbury, Suffolk CO10 6BR.

There appears to be only one competitively-selected annual scholarship available for aspiring FIs. The Norman Motley Scholarship will provide £1,500 towards the cost of a course. Applicants must meet CAA AFI experience requirements and hold the FAI/Royal Aero Club Bronze Certificate of Proficiency. Applications usually close in the spring. The trust is administered by GAPAN. Requirements for sponsorship will change in line with the JAA Flight Crew Licensing amendments in June 2000, so the Guild should be consulted as to the current qualifications.

Bear in mind that not everyone is temperamentally suited to becoming an instructor, and the financial rewards are small. The most common complaint of flying instructors the world over is that they are overworked and underpaid. The fault lies, to some extent, in the hours-building system, which spawns a ready and eager workforce of transient hours-builders, some of whom are happy to work for very low pay in return for free flying time. This does little to encourage attractive salaries for instructors, and increasingly fewer full-time career-orientated people are to be found in flying clubs. The JAA requirements may ease this slightly, but under both systems you need to be independently financed to fund the training, and training within the job, as with other occupations, is not possible. If, however, you can support yourself with another spare-time job, instructing can be the quickest way to accumulate flying time towards an ATPL.

The choice between a CAA/IR course and the self-improvement route is really no choice at all. Either you have a sponsor (or the money to pay for the full-time course) or you beaver away, accumulating flying hours as fast as you can. Which method produces the best commercial pilot? There is a feeling within the professional pilot training industry that a self-improver working up to the 700 hours minimum experience requirement is not so well-equipped for the CPL as the full-time trainee. A flying diet of 500 or 600 hours doing nothing but instructing PPL students or hauling parachutists up to altitude is hardly ideal. On the other hand, it is arguable that a pilot who can face the hard, impecunious path of hours-building from PPL to BCPL to CPL is likely to be better motivated than the sponsored student.

For those who do work their way up, abridged ground school courses are available at the professional training schools enable them to prepare for the CPL examinations. A typical course lasts eight weeks, and is timed to finish shortly before the CAA professional licence examinations are held. These courses are usually very well subscribed by 'self-improver' CPL candidates and are frequently filled a year or more in advance, so early application is advisable.

Training Abroad

One further option might be worth considering for obtaining a CPL. You may have seen in aviation magazines those tempting advertisements from American flight schools which offer 'Commercial and Instrument Tickets in Sunny Florida in Only 90 Days!' These usually quote amazingly low prices which, allowing extra for return transatlantic air fares and accommodation, promise to reduce the cost of a British CPL/IR course by as much as two-thirds. There has to be a snag – and there is. A US FAA CPL is not valid for the commercial operation of a British-registered aeroplane. In other words, it does not entitle you to earn a living by flying British aircraft in Britain. Unlike the private licence, which can usually be validated locally in foreign countries without too much fuss, there is no reciprocal arrangement whereby an American (or any other foreign) commercial licence can readily be converted to a British CPL.

The JAA licencing harmonisation in 1999 should solve the problem within the European Community, and in the very long term the USA will no doubt join the system. Until then, the CAA would consider time logged on a US commercial course and make a recommendation for further UK CPL training. For the holder of an American Commercial licence who has completed only a basic training course in the USA, this recommendation would usually call for about 180 hours further flying training, plus the full CPR/IR ground school course. So it is no shortcut, and clearly much more expensive in the final analysis. Passes in FAA ground exams are unlikely to be accepted in lieu of any of the CAA CPL examinations, nor is a GFT exemption likely, regardless of experience gained in the USA.

However, if you gain a US Commercial licence and use it to build flying hours cheaply in the USA, where aircraft hire rates are much lower than those in Britain, the hours logged (or at least a proportion of them) could be counted towards the minima for a British BCPL or CPL. The CAA's Flight Crew Licensing Department assesses such cases individually on merit, so do not believe any claim that a course offered by a US flight school guarantees exemption from British requirements (or a job!) when you get back home.

Many American flight schools offer their successful graduates a job placement service, and US Immigration Authorities do permit overseas students to work in the USA for up to twelve months after qualifying, provided they have undertaken a career-orientated course of at least six months' duration and the employment is directly related to their field of study, in this case flying. Not all of these 'jobs' are what they seem. Some corporate and third-level aircraft operators who need two-pilot crews to meet operational or insurance regulations use the flight schools as a source of low-paid, or sometimes unpaid labour. Finding even unpaid flying work in the USA may not be easy, as there are a quarter of a million licensed professional pilots in the country and many tens of thousands of improvers. You would need to have a very special ability to face such local competition.

The Job Market

What kind of employment can a newly-qualified professional pilot expect to be offered? It would be unwise to think of the licence itself as the key to a wide choice of flying schools. A freshly-issued licence, with all of 150 or 200 hours logged, is unlikely to bring prospective employers beating a path to your door. A BCPL or CPL without an IR is *very* limiting, as a CPL/IR is mandatory for the commander or copilot of any aircraft engaged in scheduled or charter public transport services. A non IR commercial pilot would be limited to a narrow choice of activities such as instructing, pleasure-flying, glider-towing, parachute-dropping, perhaps aerial photography of a non-specialised nature, acting as copilot on an aircraft not legally required to have two crews, or agricultural aviation. However, agricultural flying is a *very* specialised and skilled business, and few operators will hire pilots with less than 500 hours experience in the work.

This 'must have experience' requirement is a common stumbling block for the newly-qualified CPL. How can you gain experience without a flying job, for which you need experience? The answer, most often, is to swallow your pride, pocket your bright new BCPL or CPL and accept employment in some lesser capacity than first pilot to gain access to experience-building opportunities. In this respect a pilot who can offer some other skills outside the cockpit, such as engineer, salesman, accountant, office clerk or even van driver, might stand a better chance of attracting an employer than one who can fly, full stop. This reinforces the view that any pilot who has acquired a commercial licence *and* an NVQ qualification will be far more likely than a non-NVQ counterpart to obtain an aviation-linked job.

The CPL/IR holder is in a stronger position, because under CAA rules this licence/rating permits the holder to act as captain of light aeroplanes and to act as copilot on *any* aeroplane, although separate type ratings are required for the operation of aircraft weighing more than 5,700 kg. However, under JAA rules separate type and class ratings are required for various aircraft, regardless of weight. To captain an airliner in commercial service an ATPL is necessary as explained in the following chapter.

Setting aside airline employment, which is dealt with below, the opportunities for CPL/IRs in general aviation are varied, and air-taxi work is an obvious possibility. Most air taxi operators will require captains to have logged a minimum 1,000 hours flying time, of which 500 hours must be as pilot-in-command, but copilot positions are available to those with less experience. A fixed-base operation which offers flying instruction and *ad hoc* charter work would also be a good, though not highly-paid, starting point for a new CPL willing to instruct and undertake commercial charter flying. Similar openings occur from time to time with operators of private business aircraft.

The commercial pilot job market is cyclical, and at the time of writing is enjoying a boom. In a book of this kind it is clearly impossible to predict just where employment openings might occur at any future time, but besides the obvious source of vacancies advertised in the aviation press, trade organisations such as the Air Training Association, the Aircraft Owners and Pilots Association, the British Helicopter Advisory Board, the General Aviation Manufacturers and Traders Association, the Guild of Air Pilots and Air Navigators or the Student Pilots Association, which is dedicated to assisting those seeking to become professional pilots, (see addresses on page 137) can probably offer advice on the current situation.

Chapter 4
The Airline Pilot

In the previous chapter we touched briefly on airline flying from the licensing angle, and on the 'self-improver' route to a CPL. This chapter concentrates on the direct route to an airliner's flight deck, through sponsorship by an airline, in this case British Airways (BA).

First, to put the airline employment situation into perspective, it is necessary to return to the early post-Second World War years of civil aviation in Great Britain. Then, airlines were staffed almost without exception by ex-Service pilots, of which there was a plentiful supply. As air travel blossomed, so the need for a dedicated sponsorship scheme was identified. The two 'flag carriers', British European Airways (BEA) and the British Overseas Airways Corporation (BOAC), both now merged into BA, established the College of Air Training at Hamble in Hampshire. There the airlines trained their own sponsored cadets from *ab initio* through to CPL/IR standard, ready to begin type conversion training on the airline's own fleets. To supplement the college's output when necessary, BEA, BOAC and, later BA also sent trainees to two private-enterprise commercial flying training schools at Oxford and Perth.

The oil crisis of 1973, airline cutbacks and changing demands for travel resulted in a glut of airline pilots as newly-trained personnel joined the many ex-Service people who were still flying commercially. When the first edition of this book appeared, in 1982, BA had some 200 trained cadets who had not been offered employment after graduation from the College of Air Training, which was shortly to be closed for good. Prospects for would-be airline pilots were depressingly poor.

Yet there were those in the industry who, quite correctly, predicted a complete reversal. They had calculated that the young pilots who had joined the airlines in the early 1950s would reach their mandatory retirement age in the mid-1980s, creating a retirement 'bulge'. So in February 1987 the British national airline began advertising for applicants to sponsor for training as commercial pilots. British Airways' studies of its pilot recruitment and training policies, based on anticipated aircraft fleet numbers, estimated flying hours and crew required, suggested that the airline needed to recruit between 100 and 160 new pilots each year. The airline planned to supply 85% from sponsored trainees, making up the balance from direct-entry qualified pilots.

British Airways defined its requirements for sponsored trainees by drawing up a specification based on a profile of the best existing pilot workforce. A cross-section of captains and first officers were invited to define the qualities they considered important for doing their jobs. They acted as guinea pigs, taking aptitude and selection tests being developed for the new crop of recruits. Teams from polytechnics and sixth form colleges were also invited to take the tests, to assess how differing backgrounds, working environments and 'life experiences' were reflected in the performance of 'candidates'.

The basic requirements of the 1995 British Airways' cadet selection process are given below. Potential candidates are recommended to check the current criteria before making any commitments.

- **a** Candidates must have the right to live and work in the UK, without limit of time.
- **b** Their age must be between 18 and 28 years.
- **c** Height must be between 1.63 and 1.93 m.
- **d** Academically, the requirement is for a minimum of seven passes in GCSE, including English language, mathematics and a science subject, and two passes at Advanced Level, at 'C' grade or above.

Experience has shown that many arts-orientated cadets found difficulty in coping with ground school training slightly greater than their sciences-based colleagues. Because of schools' tendency to 'stream' students into arts or sciences disciplines after GCSE examinations, anyone hoping for a BA cadetship should be thinking of subject specialisation before taking O-Levels. This means at the age of 14–15 years, because sixth form streaming usually reflects performance in O-Level examinations.

It is worth stating here that this 'science only' emphasis is not universally shared in the airline pilot training industry. Some experienced training staff feel that the case for mathematics and physics is overstated, and that a good rounded education, perhaps with subjects such as economics at A Level, produces equally suitable airline captain material.

On the subject of graduate trainees there is more agreement. A university degree is not essential for professional pilot training courses. Because of the age limits set on potential recruits, a graduate is likely to be leaving university at the same age as a direct-entry school-leaver would be starting route flying after completing training.

The sifting process begins on receipt of an initial enquiry. As a rough guide, if 15,000 enquiries are received, 150 may prove eligible for sponsorship. Of those, as a 'worst case' average, eight might be expected to drop out during flying training. The GCSE standards alone narrow the potential 'catchment area' to the top few per cent of the education spectrum. Those who can meet the airline's exacting selection requirements will be very high-calibre individuals who could go to university or into almost any of the professions.

After initial screening for educational qualifications, age and height, those who appear appropriately qualified are invited to make formal applications. The form requests details of educational accomplishments, school, college or university activities, social and sporting interests, previous employment if any, aviation experience and 'career objectives'. For instance, why do you want to be an airline pilot? What attracts you to British Airways? What have you done with your life that might help you as a pilot, and what is your expectation of a career as an airline pilot?

As well as an interest in the technical aspects of flying, British Airways looks for its cadets to have an interest in the company as a business, in the customer service aspects of flying and in the human factors element of team working, both on the flight deck and in the wider world of the airline as a whole.

What, then, of those who select a career in airline flying as one of several possible options carrying a high salary? In the past, BA did employ some people who simply drew up a short list of desirable jobs, but the airline believes current selection processes will weed those out.

The age at which academic qualifications are attained is significant. GCSE passes achieved first time, with no re-sits, would be a plus, and an academic course leading to passes at A Level is essential. Many successful candidates also have good university degrees. Developing social skills and having played an active part in group activities and taken responsibilities are also important.

All pilots and trainees are selected on the assumption that they may become captains. The days when airline captains were aloof from the remainder of the crew are long gone. Now more than ever they are a part of a team, and the airline looks for people who can get along with their colleagues, on the flight deck and in the cabin, and with the passengers. These are the people who will be sufficiently self-confident and assertive not to hesitate to question an action on the flight deck if the need arises. In essence, airline captains are high achievers, strong socially confident leaders, possessing team skills and an awareness of the business needs of the airline.

Some of this can be gleaned from answers on the application forms, but the sorting process begins in earnest on primary assessment. Shortlisted applicants are invited to undertake initial written aptitude and ability tests that probe mental agility, critical thinking, mechanical reasoning and technical numeracy at British Airways Recruitment and Selection Centre. At the centre, candidates are tested in a computerised testing facility. The tasks comprise a series of computer-based tests to determine hand-eye co-ordination, tracking control, the ability to interpret instruments, spatial awareness, and basic motor activity. The Meadowbank facility has testing stations, each with a computer, visual display unit and miniature set of aircraft 'controls', all linked to a master instructor's console. Candidates' scores are automatically computed and printed out. Those who are successful at this stage are asked to complete a medical questionnaire and to have a medical examination (not an aviation licence medical) performed by their own doctor.

They then attend an assessment phase comprising written tests, assessment of team skills and 'personality profiling'. Discussion subjects, require nominated candidates to lead, sum up and report on each subject ensuring that everyone is given a fair chance. Group exercises, called 'structured leadership tests', are also employed. The candidates are set a problem that has a finite solution, and they have to solve it and prepare a written report on how the solution was reached. However, BA does not go in for the 'here's a plank of wood and an old tyre, now cross this shark-infested river' type of exercise. Candidates are individually assessed at two interview sessions each with a Flight Operations and a Human Resources selection specialist.

Once they are over those considerable hurdles, the final phase is to attend the CAA Medical Branch for a full Class One medical examination by CAA and BA medical staff. The disqualifying medical problems have no particular pattern, but colour blindness and childhood illnesses that have left previously undetected weaknesses are among them. Those who pass as fit can expect to receive a formal offer of sponsorship and a place on a future training course.

Candidates are then assigned to a flying training school approved by BA and the CAA. The course, which lasts about 16 months, begins with eight weeks of ground tuition. Modern facilities at the flying college include classrooms equipped with push-button answering systems linked to a 'tell-tale' panel monitored by the tutor. When questions are asked, the tutor can tell at a glance if an incorrect response has been given.

Flying training typically starts with a 55-hour course on aircraft such as Piper Warriors, devoted principally to basic handling. Cadets might then typically move on to the Swiss-built FFA Bravo. The Bravo is fully aerobatic and cleared for spinning, and is used to introduce trainees to more-advanced flying techniques and solo cross-country work. A further 60 hours of instrument training is carried out on Warriors, bringing the total single-engine experience to 155 hours. This is followed by a 45 hours multi-engine course on Piper Seneca III twins. Part of the multi-engine training is crew-orientated 'mutual' flying, with two trainees sharing cockpit duties. The aircraft are equipped with instrument panels that duplicate as far as possible the standard flight deck arrangement adopted in the airline's fleet. Some 40 hours simulator flying is included in the course, at the end of which trainees spend about a further 50 hours in jet simulators.

This phase of training is known as Line Orientated Flying Training (LOFT). Its purpose is fourfold. First, it introduces cadets to company procedures. They 'fly' standard BA schedules, which means they sometimes get calls to report for duty in the small hours, just as operational crews do, and are expected to act in every respect as line pilots. The flying colleges issue BA's computerised flight plans and meteorological briefings so that on every 'flight' trainees get used to doing things using British Airways procedures. The aim is for 'seamless' training, so that by the time newly qualified cadets arrive at the airline's simulator centre at Cranebank near Heathrow, for type conversion training, company procedures will be entirely familiar. Secondly, LOFT provides an introduction to the higher speeds at which everything happens when flying jets. Thirdly, it teaches cadets to function as a crew. Finally, it provides an opportunity for airline staff to assess the students.

The airline is dedicated to the two-crew concept. Although BA's fleet will not become entirely two-pilot until well into the 21st century (some older Boeing 747s, McDonnell Douglas DC-10s and the Concordes are expected to be operational until at least 2007), the rank of second officer has already disappeared. All new pilots now become first officers on joining the airline, and on check-out immediately fly as second-in-command.

The course lasts 70 weeks, after which graduates emerge with a CPL/IR and a 'frozen ATPL' (they will have passed the ATPL exams, but need to accumulate flying hours to reach the ATPL minima). The failure rate recorded in the first three years of training is remarkably low.

Operational training following the BA flying college course begins with a familiarisation stage, when new recruits become acquainted with the many facets of running an airline beyond the flight deck; traffic management, engineering, ticket sales, and even catering.

Once the introductory 'get-to-know-your-airline' phase is over, work begins on training for a type rating on the multi-engine jet airliners that the new pilots will fly operationally. For a newly trained ex-cadet this would normally be one of BA's short-range aircraft such as the ATP or Boeing 737 or 757, which they will fly exclusively until 'converted' to another type later in their careers. As a rule, pilots do not fly more than one aircraft type during any one phase of their careers, though they may hold type ratings for several.

Training for the type rating is conducted at Cranebank, where BA has the latest audio-visual training aids, cockpit procedures trainers and full-motion computer-generated-image flight simulators for all of the aircraft in its fleet except the ATP, Airbus A320 and Concorde. The simulator for the supersonic aircraft is owned by co-manufacturer British Aerospace at its Bristol-Filton factory. British Airways has CAA approval for Level 4 'zero flight time' type ratings on several of its simulators. This means that experienced pilots can be type-rated on the aircraft solely on simulator practice, and may fly the actual aircraft for the first time on a scheduled service.

After a three-month conversion course at Cranebank, new pilots are released to the line as copilots under supervision, in which role they must fly a minimum of 45 sectors and pass route checks before being cleared as fully qualified copilots. From the start of training to operational flying takes slightly less than two years.

The first opportunity to change aircraft type is likely to occur after some five years of line flying. Pilots can 'bid' for crew vacancies on other aircraft fleets, moving up to larger short-haul or long-haul aircraft such as the Boeing 757, 767 or 747. If successful, they undergo further conversion training to gain the new type rating.

It is reasonable to assume that everyone who embarks on a career as an airline pilot eventually seeks the coveted left-hand seat of an airliner, the captain's position. Equally, when selecting recruits and throughout the continual training process that is part of every pilot's life, the airlines view every pilot as a potential future captain. They do not mark certain trainees as lifetime co-pilots and others as captains; in theory everyone selected has the stuff of command within, but obviously not everyone can achieve the ultimate ambition.

The command structure is based on seniority, but becoming a captain is not automatic. British Airways regards the midpoint of a pilot's career as the appropriate time to consider promotion to captain on short-range aircraft. As a probationary captain, a pilot would have to demonstrate to a training captain the ability to make sound, commercially viable, operationally safe decisions, and to direct and co-ordinate the work of flight crew, cabin crew and ground staff over many flights before being granted full command. After three to five years in command, an opportunity might arise to switch aircraft types. The ideal career structure in the airline's view is to fly as copilot on two or three types of aircraft and then, following a mid-career promotion to captain, follow the same pattern in command.

Other sponsors

The Amy Johnson Memorial Trust and Airtour International offer an open competition scholarship worth up to £1,500 to assist PPL holders towards the cost of their first professional licence, BCPL, CPL, or ATPL. Candidates must be female, British subjects, permanently resident in the UK, and have a date of birth on or after 1 January 1955. There are various other conditions, but pilots who hold or have held AFI, FI, restricted BCPL, BCPL, CPL or ATPL ratings are not eligible. Under the JAA harmonisation changes due to come into effect in July 1999, the sponsorship towards a BCPL will no longer apply.

The closing date for this year (1998) has already passed, and applications for 1999 should be made before 17 February 1999 (and the same date each subsequent year) to the Honorary Secretary to the Trust, Mrs M E Tucker, 12 Church Lane, Merton Park, London SW19 3PD. Her telephone number is 0181 540 1797.

Apart from BA, several other British airlines offer (or have in the past offered) sponsorship schemes, although the cyclical nature of the airline pilot job market makes it impossible to predict when trainees may be recruited.

British Midland Airways and Britannia Airways operate Bursary Sponsorship schemes with the Oxford Air Training School which involve the trainee paying part of the cost (around 50% in two parts, some of which may be deducted in instalments from eventual salary) of training to CPL/IR standard, with the airline paying the balance and offering a five-year contracted flight deck position once the trainee has qualified. Age limits are 18–26, with much the same educational and other selection criteria as applied by BA, and courses are run twice a year. Details of these schemes may be obtained from the Bursary Selection Office, Oxford Air Training School, Oxford Airport, Kidlington OX5 1RA.

Another possibility, though more suited to 'self-improvers', is the Joint Sponsorship Scheme operated by the Cabair Group of companies in conjunction with Air UK. It is open to those aged 18–31 who hold a PPL with IMC Rating and 150 flying hours logged. Selected applicants pay around £6,000 towards the cost of getting a basic CPL, after which they work for about two years as flying instructors with the Cabair Group's flying schools before joining Air UK as first officers, with some 1,000 flying hours logged and two years' aviation work experience behind them. The Cabair Group also operates its own sponsorship scheme, for which the applicant's input is around £10,000. Any pilot considering this, or any similar scheme, may be entitled to full income tax relief by registering for the NVQ in Piloting Transport Aircraft. A similar partially sponsored scheme is operated by the London Flight Centre at Lydd Airport. It offers selected *ab initio* candidates a course that results in a CPL/IR, a 'frozen' ATPL and a flying instructor's rating with about 700 hours flight time. The 18 to 20-month course costs the candidate about £20,000, less some £4,000 earned as a flying instructor during the training. They also offer the possibility of post-qualification positions as copilots or captains of commercial aircraft operated by associated companies.

Apart from direct sponsorship schemes such as those outlined, airlines recruit pilots from two principal sources; a pool of commercially-licensed pilots working for other airlines or in other branches of civil aviation such as flying instruction and air taxi work, and from the armed services.

What are the chances of a 'self-improver' Commercial pilot getting an airline job? It naturally depends on the state of the job market at the time, but in recent years the growth in regional air services and 'third-level' carriers, often operating relatively unsophisticated twin-turboprop aircraft, has increased both the opportunities for employment and the demand for commercial pilot training courses. At the beginning of the 1990s opportunities for employment were grim, at the time of writing, 1998, airlines are scratching round to fill their vacancies. One major carrier is rumoured to be interviewing anyone with a car driving licence. Historically however, as soon as all these posts are filled the employment market will then suffer a surplus of qualified pilots unlikely to find a position.

Nonetheless, examples of successful self-improvers who have reached airliner flight decks are not that hard to find. One (modestly anonymous) woman pilot was flying as a first officer three years after taking a trial flying lesson. She managed to borrow the cost of a PPL course (but only after applying to several bank managers who considered her ambition to become a professional pilot unrealistic), completed the course in a month and worked a further six months in a non-flying job to pay off the debt. Another period of employment with an aviation company earned a modest salary, but included about 2 hours free flying each week, and with more help from an understanding bank manager she took an Instructor's Rating course which enabled her to build hours towards a CPL and IR. Three years after first handling an aircraft's controls she was copiloting a Shorts 330 commuter airliner.

Her story is hardly unique, but remember that, apart from a mandatory CPL/IR, the minimum experience level which any airline will normally set before considering a pilot is 1,000 hours subject to the applicant successfully meeting other criteria (motivation, character, performance, medical and psychological suitability) as applied to *ab initio* recruits. A common thread which runs through every success story of self-improvers attaining an airline position is dedication to achieving that goal. There are no guarantees, no short-cuts. The route is long, arduous, expensive in time and money, and often dispiriting, but for those who make it (and it has to be said that many do not) it is ultimately very rewarding.

Chapter 5

The Military Pilot

A career with the armed services offers some of the finest pilot training and certainly the most exciting flying in the world. Competition for a trainee pilot's position is thus extremely fierce and the selection procedures are rigorous, and with good cause, for the cost of training a Royal Air Force fast-jet pilot to squadron service standard is more than £3 million. Small wonder, then, that for every 200 enquiries received from aspiring Service pilots, on average only one will successfully negotiate the selection and training procedures described below to become an RAF pilot.

The RAF recruits aircrew officers either directly (from school, polytechnic, university or civilian life) or via an RAF-sponsored university cadetship scheme. A major change in recruitment policy was announced in July 1989, following a study which recommended broadening the opportunities for women in the service. They became eligible to serve as RAF pilots and navigators for the first time since its formation in 1918. Women pilots, the first of whom began training in early 1990, will be permitted to fly fast jets, combat helicopters, transports, tankers, airborne early warning and search-and-rescue aircraft, and to serve as flying instructors. Target recruitment is for an annual total of 270 RAF pilots, of whom up to 15% may be women.

The Royal Air Force

The minimum age and educational requirements for RAF aircrew entrants are as follows. School-leavers, graduates, civilians must be aged between 17½–24 years on entry, though application must be made before reaching the age of 23½. They must have at least two passes at A Level plus GCSE Ordinary Level (or equivalent) at Grade C or above, in English language and mathematics. Applicants must be subjects or citizens of Great Britain or the Republic of Ireland, or must have been born in a country which is (or was) within the British Commonwealth or Republic of Ireland, or have both parents who meet (or met) those qualifications. In exceptional circumstances a dispensation against these requirements may be made at the discretion of the Secretary of State for Defence, but all applicants must possess British nationality at the time of application, and applicants not of UK origin must normally have been resident in the UK for a minimum period of five years.

As part of the RAF's Graduate Entry Scheme, sponsorships are available to undergraduates and prospective undergraduates taking full-time degree courses at a recognised UK educational establishment. RAF University Cadetship awards lead to permanent commissions in the Service and attract a starting salary of some £11,000 per annum. In addition, university fees are paid by the RAF. Bursary awards are also available, but without fees payment or prejudice to local education authority grants, and lead to short service commissions.

University Air Squadrons

Before examining the RAF's selection and training procedures, it is worth looking at the role of the University Air Squadrons (UASs). Lord Trenchard conceived the idea of forming Air Squadrons at the Oxford and Cambridge Universities in 1919, with the declared object of 'encouraging an interest in flying, and promoting and maintaining liaison with universities in technical and research problems affecting aviation . . . (and) to assist those who wished to take up aeronautics as a profession, either in the Royal Air Force or in a civilian capacity, and those who, while not making aviation their career, desired to give part-time service to defence in the non-regular air force'.

That is precisely the function of the 16 UASs (listed on pages 96–8) which exists today under direct command of the Director Elementary Flying Training Headquarters, University and Air Cadets, at the RAF College at Cranwell in Lincolnshire. The 17th UAS, the Royal Military Air College at Shrivenham, conducts non-flying training. UASs form the largest flying training organisation within the RAF, and are affiliated to about 80 universities and university colleges throughout the British Isles.

There are three classes of University Air Squadron membership; RAF Volunteer Reserve (RAF(VR)) members, University Bursars and University Cadets. RAF Volunteer Reservists are undergraduates who want to learn to fly but initially are under no obligation to join the RAF. Recruitment is usually carried out within the first week of a new university year, and applications exceed available places by a factor of four or five to one. Women undergraduates were permitted to join UASs from 1985, and now comprise some 15% of total UAS strength nationwide. RAF(VR) members are entlisted as Aircraftsmen (or Women) but enjoy the status of Officer Cadets. While they do not have to undergo the rigorous aptitude tests which RAF aircrew entrants must take, RAF(VR) members must pass medical and selection boards before flying service aircraft. RAF(VR) membership of UASs is normally limited to one year, but may be extended for a further year to those seriously interested in pursuing a flying career with the RAF.

University Bursar and University Cadet UAS members are sponsored by the RAF following acceptance by the Department of Officer Recruitment and selection at the RAF College, Cranwell. University Bursars are committed to Short Service Commissions with the RAF after university graduation. University Cadets are commissioned and paid as acting pilot officers while studying, and after graduation enter the Service as junior officers. All RAF-sponsored undergraduates, including those destined for careers in the ground branches of the service, automatically become UAS members.

In a typical UAS, RAF(VR) members outnumber University Bursars and University Cadets by more than two to one. The number of University Cadets within the total UAS flying membership is currently set at 725. Individual squadron membership varies from 40–80, according to the number and size of educational establishments served. The geographic spread of UASs is such that few major educational centres are denied access to a squadron within an acceptable travelling distance.

The UAS pilot training course provides for 30 hours per year over three years. For RAF(VR) members completing the Basic Course, 40 hours training is often sufficient to qualify them for a civilian PPL after taking the relevant CAA examinations and flight tests, without completing a civilian PPL course. However, this is not an aim of UAS membership, and issue of a civilian licence is at the discretion of the CAA.

UAS flying courses are conducted on a fleet of 80 Scottish Aviation Bulldog T Mk. 1 two-seat trainers. The Basic Course syllabus comprises general handling and circuit procedures leading to first solo (usually after 11 hours dual instruction), instrument training and navigation. Students' progress is closely monitored and tested at 'critical points', each of which must be passed satisfactorily before moving on to the next stage of training. After 35–40 hours students must take a Basic Handling Test, which equates approximately to the experience level required for a civilian PPL and should be within reach of all UAS students. The much-prized RAF Preliminary Flying Badge is typically awarded at 70–80 hours, and is thus generally only achievable by Long Course students or university-sponsored students staying in the UAS for a third year's flying. Long Course students, who include all University Cadets destined for pilot careers in the service, also learn instrument flying procedures, aerobatics and formation flying, bringing them up to Cranwell Entry Standard (CES).

The UASs provide an excellent opportunity for young people to experience flying in a Service environment. Military discipline has to be observed and uniform worn, and a substantial commitment of time is demanded, typically one or two half-days each week during term time for flying training, and one evening per week for ground studies. However, care is taken to ensure that over-enthusiastic pilots do not neglect their academic studies in favour of flying! During the university or polytechnic summer vacations, UASs deploy to RAF stations for a four-week summer camp devoted to concentrated flying and gaining an insight into Service life. In addition there is a wide range of sporting and social activities and inter-squadron competitions to be enjoyed.

The following University Air Squadrons are currently active:

Squadron	Academic Institutions served	Base
Aberdeen, Dundee and St Andrews UAS	Aberdeen University; Dundee University; Robert Gordon University; St Andrews University; University of Abertay, Dundee	RAF Leuchars
Birmingham UAS	Aston University; Birmingham University; Coventry University; Keele University; Staffordshire University; University of Wolverhampton; University of Central England in Birmingham; Warwick University	RAF Cosford
Bristol UAS	Bath University; Bristol University; Exeter University; Plymouth University; University of the West of England at Bristol	RAF Colerne

An instrument rating student using a flight simulator for procedures practice, with instructor at left monitoring his progress on a plotter. (Wycombe Air Centre)

Beech Super King Air 350, a typical air taxi and corporate aircraft on which commercial pilots may find positions as co-pilots. (Mike Jerram)

The Shorts 360 twin-turboprop commuter airliner is widely used throughout the world on 'third-level' routes. (Shorts)

This Gates Learjet 35A operated by Manchester-based Northern Executive Aviation marks the upper end of the air-taxi market. (NEA)

The co-pilot's position on British Airways' large fleet of Boeing 737s will be the first place of work for many of the airline's newly trained pilots. (BA)

The ultimate assignment? British Airways' Concorde. (BA)

Increasing use of helicopters for police surveillance and emergency duties has created new *opportunities for experienced ex-military helicopter pilots.*

The RAF Air Cadets organisation, which has given thousands of youngsters their first experience of flying, is re-equipping with these German-built Grob 109B Vigilant motor gliders. (Paul Jackson)

Cambridge UAS	Anglia Polytechnic; Cambridge University; University of East Anglia; University of Essex	Cambridge Airport
East Lowlands UAS	Edinburgh University; Heriot-Watt University; Napier University; Stirling University	RAF Turnhouse
East Midlands UAS	De Montford University; Nottingham University; Leicester University; Loughborough University of Technology; Nottingham Trent University	RAF Newton
Glasgow and Strathclyde UAS	Glasgow University; Glasgow Caledonian University; Strathclyde University; University of Paisley	Glasgow Airport
Liverpool UAS	Lancaster University; Liverpool University; Liverpool John Moores University; University of Central Lancashire	RAF Woodvale
University of London UAS	Brunel University; Canterbury College, Kent; City University; Greenwich University; Hertfordshire University; Kingston University; London University; University of Kent	RAF Benson
Manchester and Salford UAS	Manchester University Salford University; University of Manchester Institute of Science & Technology (UMIST); Manchester Metropolitan University	RAF Woodvale
Northumbrian UAS	Durham University; Newcastle University; University of Northumbria at Newcastle; University of Sunderland; University of Teeside	RAF Leeming
Oxford UAS	Oxford Brookes University; Oxford University; Reading University	RAF Benson
Queens UAS	Queens University of Belfast; University of Ulster at Coleraine and Jordanstown Sites; Stanmillis College, Belfast	Belfast (Sydenham) Airport
Southampton UAS	Southampton University; University of Portsmouth	RAF Boscombe Down
University of Wales UAS	St David's University College, Lampeter; University College of Wales, Aberystwyth; University of Glamorgan; University of Wales College of Cardiff; University College of North Wales;	RAF St Athan

	University College of Swansea; University of Wales College of Medicine	
Yorkshire UAS	Bradford University; Hull University; Leeds Metropolitan University; Leeds University; Sheffield Hallam University; Sheffield University; University of Huddersfield; University of Humberside; York University	RAF Church Fenton

For details of individual UASs, contact the individual university, college or polytechnic direct or write to: The Officer Commanding, University Air Squadrons, RAF Cranwell, Sleaford, Lincolnshire NG34 8HB.

Selecting Aircrew for the Royal Air Force

Direct Entrants and University Cadets both begin their RAF careers with an application to the Officer and Aircrew Selection Centre (OASC) at RAF College Cranwell. Application is made on a six-part form, RAF Form 6520, which has sections for personal, educational, previous employment, recreation, previous military service, flying experience and general information.

The selection of potential aircrew is carried out by The Air Board, and the four-part selection process at Cranwell takes four days. Applicants arrive at Cranwell on a Sunday for briefings and orientation. On the second day candidates take aptitude tests aimed at finding out how each will respond to aircrew training, measuring their ability to learn rather than their ability to perform at this stage.

The OASC uses computer-based aptitude tests for prospective aircrew, in place of earlier electro-mechanical devices. Fifty-three individual computer monitors/keyboard stations are used to test applicants for all the British Services and some overseas forces, with an annual throughput of 8,000 potential pilots, navigators and controllers.

The computer equipment analyses a candidate's co-ordination of hand, eye and foot; rate control; instrument interpretation; spatial awareness; memory, deductive reasoning; selective attention; information scheduling and perceptual speed, all of which are valuable pointers to his ability to fly, navigate and fight in a modern jet aircraft. After some 11 tests have been completed, the computer gives examiners an instant analysis which enables them to determine a candidate's suitability for further testing as a possible pilot (or navigator, or controller) trainee. On the third day candidates undergo a thorough medical examination and a 45 minute character assessment interview conducted by two RAF officers. Candidates who have passed the aptitude tests, the medical, and show promise at the interview are selected to take part in 'syndicate tests'. Each 'syndicate' consists of a team of five or six candidates who are supplied with numbered overall suits to preserve their anonymity. The syndicate is boarded by two officers who assess the candidate through five different exercises: Practical Team, Discussion, Planning (Theoretical), an Individual Theoretical Problem and Individually Led Practical. The idea is that the subsequent conversations will reveal how each applicant responds to others, whether he or she mixes easily or is reticent, and whether he/she is a leader or a follower. The syndicate is set a planning exercise in which a specific task is outlined, and the candidates must draw up a plan of action and justify their decisions. The final round of team tests consists of a practical exercise (for example, crossing a hangar floor without touching the ground, using only a couple of planks and some suspended motor tyres), which looks like a practice session for the Royal Tournament. This is aimed at assessing qualities of leadership, courage, judgement, enthusiasm, initiative and determination.

Those who complete the selection course satisfactorily can usually expect to hear whether they have been accepted for aircrew entry or a university cadetship within a month of their visit to the OASC. Rejected applicants may re-apply for further assessment at the OASC provided they have not exceeded the maximum age limits for entry. At least 12 months must elapse before subsequent re-application. Those who fail the flying aptitude tests may be invited to consider non-aircrew careers if they have opted for alternatives on their initial applications.

Aircrew Training

Once selected, new aircrew recruits for the RAF undergo an 18-week Initial Officer Training course at the RAF College at Cranwell in Lincolnshire. The IOT course prepares entrants for their responsibilities as junior RAF officers. It includes drill routine, assault courses, initiative tests, survival training and general physical activities such as canoeing and mountain climbing.

After IOT, direct entrants with no previous flying experience undergo 63 hours basic training in Slingsby Firefly training aircraft at the Joint Elementary Flying Training School, RAF Barkston Heath.

The Basic Flying Training course is conducted at No 1 Flying Training school, RAF Linton-on-Ouse. The 32-week course consists of four weeks ground school, 50 hours in a simulator and 120 hours flying. Trainees can expect to solo about three weeks into the course.

On completion of the Basic Flying Training course, pilots are 'streamed' for the type of operational aircraft for which they are considered best suited: Group 1 (fast jet), Group 2 (multi-engine), or Group 3 (helicopters). Most newly-trained pilots are streamed for fast jets, since this is the RAF's primary operational requirement.

These totals of hours include a flexibility element to permit additional flying according to individual trainees' needs, and a further incidental allowance provides for the completion of aborted flying sorties, test failures, or any lack of continuity in the training programme.

The Advanced Training phase is conducted according to the Group for which pilots have been streamed. Those destined for fast jets, who will eventually fly Harriers, Jaguars or Tornadoes in squadron service, take a 100 hours advanced flying training course on British Aerospace Hawk T Mk. 1s at No 4 Flying Training School (FTS), RAF Valley. This includes tactical and weapons training before they move on to an Operational Conversion Unit (OCU) to train on the actual type of first-line aircraft to be flown on a squadron.

In time of crisis the OCUs would play an active role, either as reinforcements for other squadrons operating the same type of aircraft, or by assuming squadron status, to which end some have 'shadow squadron' status (see the following list).

After basic training, Group 2 pilots undergo a further 27 hours, eight-week course on Tucano T Mk. 1s before transferring to No 6 FTS at RAF Finningley for a 45 hours, eight-week course on British Aerospace Jetstream T Mk. 1 twin-turboprop trainers. Group 3 pilots go straight to No 2 FTS at RAF Shawbury to complete 28 weeks' rotary-wing training, comprising 76 hours on Westland Gazelle HT Mk. 3 and 50 hours on Westland Wessex HC Mk. 2 helicopters. In each case, conversion training at an appropriately-equipped OCU follows.

The complete RAF training pattern is illustrated by the following list:

RAF Training and Operational Conversion Units

Unit	Aircraft type(s)	Station
Joint Elementary Flying Training School	Firefly	RAF Barkston Heath
No 1 FTS	Tucano T Mk. 1	RAF Linton-on-Ouse
No 2 FTS	Gazelle HT Mk.3, Wessex HC Mk. 2	RAF Shawbury
No 4 FTS	Hawk T Mk. 1	RAF Valley
No 6 FTS	Dominie T Mk. 1, Jetstream T Mk. 1 Tucano T Mk. 1	RAF Finningley
226 OCU	Jaguar GR Mk. 1A/T Mk. 2A	RAF Lossiemouth
20 Squadron	Harrier GR Mk. 7/T Mk .4/T Mk. 10	RAF Wittering
27 Squadron	Chinook HC Mk. 1, Puma HC, Mk. 1	RAF Odiham
42 Squadron	Nimrod MR Mk. 2	RAF Kinloss
55 Squadron	TriStar K Mk 1, VC10 C Mk. 1/K Mk. 2/3, BAe 146 CC Mk. 2	RAF Brize Norton
56 Squadron	Tornado F Mk. 3	RAF Coningsby
57 Squadron	Hercules C Mk. 1/3	RAF Lyneham
Trinational Tornado Training Establishment	Tornado GR Mk. 1/1T	RAF Cottesmore
Tornado Weapons Conversion Unit	Tornado GR Mk. 1	RAF Honington
SAR Training Squadron	Wessex HC Mk. 2	RAF Valley

Central Flying School (Training of QFIs) operates Bulldog T Mk. 1s (RAF Cranwell), Tucano T Mk. 1s (RAF Topcliffe) and Hawk T Mk. 1 As (RAF Valley), and Gazelle HT Mk. 3 helicopters (RAF Shawbury).

Direct Entrant aircrew recruits assume the rank of Aircraftman (Officer Cadet) on entering the RAF, while graduates are commissioned as Pilot Officers. There are two types of RAF Commission. A Permanent Commission, subject to satisfactory completion of all training phases, is to the age of 55, with an optional retirement date at the earliest age of 38 or after completion of 16 years commissioned service, whichever comes later. It carries a pension which is index-linked from the age of 55. Short Service Commissions, which are not overly emphasised by the RAF for pilot entrants because of the high cost of training and current pilot shortages, are for 12 years, with an option to leave with a tax-free gratuity after eight years.

Promotion to Flying Officer and thence to Flight Lieutenant is automatic. A graduate entrant will typically reach the rank of Flight

Lieutenant within two years of entry, and could be considered for promotion to the rank of Squadron Leader after his first tour of squadron duty, although such a promotion would not be likely to be granted immediately. A Direct Entrant takes about six years to achieve the rank of Flight Lieutenant. Promotion beyond that rank is subject to written examinations, with promotions decided on the merit of annual performance reports from squadron commanders.

Promotion to the rank of Squadron Leader and beyond can only be offered to holders of Permanent Commissions. There is also a Reserve Service requirement of four years additional service in the event of recall during a national emergency. The Permanent Commission carries a pension and a tax-free gratuity equal to three times the annual pension after 16 years of service. The RAF promotion ladder looks like this:

Pilot Officer
Flying Officer
Flight Lieutenant
Squadron Leader
Wing Commander
Group Captain
Air Commodore
Air Vice-Marshal
Air Marshal
Air Chief Marshal
Marshal of the RAF

Squadron Service

At the end of his operational conversion, the newly-trained RAF pilot gets his first appointment (known as a 'posting') to an operational RAF squadron, which is the Service's basic working unit. Pilots do get an opportunity to state a preference to a particular posting, but there is no guarantee that personal wishes can be accommodated. Tours of duty (the period between postings) usually last about 30 months. To give some idea of the scope of the RAF in the 1990s and the geographical spread of operational squadrons within RAF Strike Command, the list below provides details of squadrons, the aircraft they operate and their regular bases. However, continuing defence cuts following the lessening of East-West tension and the aftermath of the Gulf War may substantially alter the pattern of

RAF overseas deployments in the future. Strike Command is responsible for strike/attack and offensive support; air defence; reconnaissance; maritime patrol and antisubmarine attack; search and rescue; transport; aerial refuelling and helicopter operations.

Squadron	**Aircraft type(s)**	**Station**
No 1	Harrier GR 7	RAF Wittering
No 2	Tornado GR 1A	RAF Marham
No 3	Harrier GR 7	RAF Laarbruch (Germany)
No 4	Harrier GR 7	RAF Laarbruch (Germany)
No 5	Tornado F 3	RAF Coningsby
No 6	Jaguar G 1A	RAF Coltishall
No 7	Chinook HC 1	RAF Odiham
No 8	Boeing Sentry AEW 1	RAF Waddington
No 9	Tornado GR 1	RAF Brüggen (Germany)
No 10	VC10 C 1	RAF Brize Norton
No 11	Tornado F 3	RAF Leeming
No 12	Tornado GR 1	RAF Lossiemouth
No 13	Tornado GR 1A	RAF Marham
No 14	Tornado GR 1	RAF Brüggen (Germany)
No 17	Tornado GR 1	RAF Brüggen (Germany)
No 18	Chinook HC 1	RAF Laarbruch (Germany)
No 19	Hawks	RAF Valley
No 20	Tornado GR 1	RAF Laarbruch (Germany)
No 22	Wessex HC 2	RAF Finningley and detachments
No 24	Hercules C 1/C 3	RAF Lyneham
No 25	Tornado F 3	RAF Leeming
No 29	Tornado F 3	RAF Coningsby
No 30	Hercules C 1/C 3	RAF Lyneham
No 31	Tornado GR 1	RAF Brüggen (Germany)
No 32	BAe 125 C 1/C 2/C 3, Gazelle HT 3/HC 4	RAF Northolt
No 33	Puma HC 1	RAF Odiham
No 39	Canberra	RAF Marham
No 41	Jaguar GR 1A	RAF Coltishall
No 42(S)	Nimrod MR 2	RAF Kinloss
No 43	Tornado F 3	RAF Leuchars
No 47	Hercules C 1/C 3	RAF Lyneham
No 51	Nimrod R 1	RAF Waddington
No 54	Jaguar GR 1A	RAF Coltishall
No 56	Tornado F 3	RAF Coningsby
No 70	Hercules C 1/C 3	RAF Lyneham
No 72	Wessex HC 2	Aldergrove Airport, Northern Ireland

No 74	Hawks	RAF Valley
No 78	Chinook HC 1, Sea King HAR 3	Mount Pleasant (Falkland Islands)
No 84	Wessex HU 5C	RAF Akrotiri (Cyprus)
No 100	Hawks	RAF Finningley
No 101	VC10 K 2/3	RAF Brize Norton
No 111	Tornado F 3	RAF Leuchars
No 120	Nimrod MR 2	RAF Kinloss
No 201	Nimrod MR 2	RAF Finningley and detachments
No 206	Nimrod MR 2	RAF Kinloss
No 208	Hawks	RAF Valley
No 216	TriStar K 1/KC 1	RAF Brize Norton
No 230	Puma HC 1	RAF Aldergrove
No 617	Tornado GR 1	RAF Lossiemouth

(S)=Shadow Squadron

The Air Training Corps

The Air Training Corps (ATC), motto *Venture Adventure*, was formed in 1941 to provide pre-entry training for boys planning careers in the RAF or Fleet Air Arm (FAA). After the war the ATC was remodelled and its scope expanded. Its present-day function is as a national voluntary youth organisation open to both boys and girls. It exists to encourage a practical interest in aviation, adventure and sport which will be useful in both Service and civilian life.

The age limits for joining the ATC are 13 to 18 years, though cadets can remain in the corps until they reach the age of 20, after which many become staff or instructors within the corps. The establishment of the ATC is for a maximum of 40,000 cadets supervised by up to 9,000 adult staff, administered from Headquarters Air Cadets at RAF Cranwell at Sleaford, in Lincolnshire. There are seven ATC regions:

Region	**Headquarters**
Scotland	RAF Turnhouse
North & East	RAF Linton-on-Ouse
Central & East	RAF Henlow
London & South East	RAF Northolt
South West	RAF Locking
Wales	RAF St Athan
North & West	RAF Sealand

These regions administer 40 Wings and approximately 1,000 Squadrons and Detached Flights. A principal function of the ATC is to provide flying experience for ATC cadets and for cadets from the CCF (RAF), via the RAF's Air Experience Flights (AEFs – see below), and Volunteer Gliding Schools. Twenty-eight such schools make the Air Cadet Gliding Organisation the largest glider training organisation in the world.

The AEFs are located at RAF Manston, Bournemouth International Airport, Colerne Airfield, Exeter Airport, Cambridge Airport, RAF Benson, RAF Newton, RAF Shawbury, RAF Finningley, RAF Woodvale, RAF Leeming, RAF Turnhouse and Belfast City Airport. Their fleet of powered aircraft is made up of de Havilland Chipmunks and British Aerospace Bulldogs. The AEFs' aim is to give each eligible ATC or CCF cadet an annual flight of 20–25 minutes. In addition, two-week courses on navigation are held each year for some 75 selected senior cadets.

The Air Cadet Gliding Organisation has a fleet of 53 all-composite Grob G.109B Vigilant Mk. 1s and 91 Grob 103 Viking gliders for training and solo flying, plus four ASW-19 Valiant and two Janus C high-performance sailplanes for advanced soaring and competition flying. The fleet is dispersed at the Air Corps Central Gliding School at RAF Syerston and at the Volunteer Gliding Schools listed below. Each year some 1,200 ATC and CCF cadets complete glider training to solo standard and gain their wings (after their 16th birthday) on the Air Cadets Gliding Organisation fleet. Another 1,400 cadets complete an initial gliding course and gain their wings.

ATC Gliding Organisation Schools

Number of school	Location
Central Gliding School	RAF Syerston, Nottinghamshire
611 VGS	Swanton Morley, Norfolk
612 VGS	Abingdon, Oxfordshire
613 VGS	Halton, Buckinghamshire
614 VGS	Wethersfield, Essex
615 VGS	Kenley, Surrey
616 VGS	Henlow, Bedfordshire
617 VGS	Manston, Kent
618 VGS	Challock, Kent
621 VGS	Hullavington, Wiltshire
622 VGS	Upavon, Wiltshire

624 VGS	Chivenor, Devon
625 VGS	Hullavington, Wiltshire
626 VGS	Predannack, Cornwall
631 VGS	Sealand, Cheshire
632 VGS	Tern Hill, Shropshire
633 VGS	Cosford, Shropshire
634 VGS	St Athan, South Glamorgan
635 VGS	Samlesbury, Lancashire
636 VGS	Swansea, West Glamorgan
637 VGS	Little Rissington, Gloucestershire
642 VGS	Linton-on-Ouse, Yorkshire
643 VGS	Syerston, Nottinghamshire
644 VGS	Syerston, Nottinghamshire
645 VGS	Catterick, Yorkshire
661 VGS	Kirknewton, Lothian
662 VGS	Arbroath, Tayside
663 VGS	Kinloss, Morayshire
664 VGS	Northern Ireland

Besides the AEFs and Volunteer Gliding Schools, the ATC operates several other schemes for getting cadets into the air. An Opportunity Flights Scheme, run with commercial airlines, enables cadets to 'sit in' on scheduled services when space permits, and several hundred cadets make such flights each year. The Overseas Flights Scheme provides an opportunity for cadets to travel on RAF transport flights on TriStar and VC10 aircraft, usually on routes to Cyprus, Germany and Gibraltar. Other *ad hoc* opportunity flights are arranged in Service aircraft, airliners and company-owned and private aeroplanes.

Perhaps the most important of the flying schemes is the Ministry of Defence (formerly RAF and Royal Navy) Flying Scholarship which provides 20 hours free flying instruction at selected civilian flying schools. Some 25–30 flying schools and clubs participate in the scheme, which is the largest sponsored flying programme in the UK. To apply for a scholarship one need not necessarily be a member of the ATC or CCF. Since the autumn of 1989 young women applicants have been accepted because of the RAF's new policy to recruit female pilots and navigators. The broad requirements are that applicants should have reached the age of 17 years by the start of their training courses, which are conducted between April and March; should hold GCSE or equivalent passes at Ordinary Level in English language, mathematics and three other subjects, only one of which may be non-academic; and can take up the offer of training within 12 months.

Shortlisted candidates undergo a 1½-day pre-assessment screening at the OASC at RAF Cranwell, where medical fitness and personal and pilot aptitudes are examined to the same standard required for entry into the RAF as aircrew. Those who pass the OASC selection procedure enter the Final Selection Competition.

The 20-hour scholarship course takes about 18 days to complete, and includes about 5 hours of solo flying in modern light training aircraft. The cost of the flying instruction and board and lodging is paid by the Ministry of Defence (MoD). Those who successfully complete the course and pass the flying tests and ground examinations receive a certificate (cadets also receive a Flying Scholarship 'wings' badge). They may then continue with their training at their own expense to complete the necessary minimum 40 hours (subject to review) for the issue of a civilian PPL.

The number of MoD scholarships awarded each year averages 500, and about two-thirds of the scholarship winners go on to obtain their PPLs. The MoD Flying Scholarship scheme does not impose any obligation on successful candidates to join the RAF, nor does it offer any guarantee of subsequent acceptance for service flying training. Another flying opportunity for Air Cadets is the Pilot Navigation Training Scheme, which provides a two-week course including 10 hours flying training on Chipmunks with an AEF.

The Royal Navy

Royal Navy admissions for trainee pilots are scarce and applicants are short-listed to only the very best, even before being seen by the interview board. The rumour that successful applicants are capable of flight with or without an aircraft are officially denied.

However, like commercial pilot vacancies, these gluts and shortages can be cyclical. Do not be deterred from investigating the current situation. Like the RAF, the RN also has a two-tier system for recruiting aircrew officers, either through the Dartmouth Naval College in Devon or by direct Graduate entry. Nationality requirements are the same as those for the RAF detailed above, but the RN's entry-age limits for trainee pilots are 17–26 years of age, and candidates must also be between 162–198 cm tall (and have 'teeth adequate for the efficient mastication of food', it says on the application form!). Initial aptitude testing for would-be navy pilots is again conducted at the OASC at RAF Cranwell, and is followed by a two-day selection session with the Admiralty Interview Board at HMS *Sultan* (a shore base, not a ship) at Gosport in Hampshire. Those candidates recommended for a commission undergo a medical examination by the Central Air Medical Board at nearby Fareham. The final selection of short-listed applicants is made by the MoD's final Selection Committee, which convenes some six to eight weeks before each point of entry to the Britannia Naval College at Dartmouth.

Those recruits who enter the Service via the Naval College assume the rank of Midshipman. Graduates take the rank of Acting Sub-Lieutenant. Both categories of entrant follow the same initial training pattern, spending two terms at Dartmouth undergoing practical training at sea, and gaining air experience on Grob 115D trainers at Plymouth Airport before starting their Elementary Flying Training (EFT) course which is conducted on Firefly trainers of the Civilian Joint Elementary Flying Training School at RAF Cranwell. The EFT course lasts 20 weeks and provides 67 hours of training.

Because the number of fixed-wing, carrier-based aircraft in the RN's inventory has been much reduced, most Fleet Air Arm pilots now fly helicopters, and there are very limited opportunities for fixed-wing pilots for the BAe Sea Harrier short take-off/vertical landing jets which serve aboard the RN's three aircraft carriers, HMS *Illustrious, Invincible* and *Ark Royal*.

Royal Navy pilots streamed for Harrier flying move from RAF Topcliffe to Cranwell for training on RAF Tucanos before proceeding to RAF Valley for advanced training and weapons training on BAe Hawks, and finally to RNAS Yeovilton for conversion and operational training on the Sea Harrier F/A 2.

Helicopter pilots move from RAF Topcliffe to RNAS Culdrose in Cornwall for a further 18-week, 80-hour training course on Westland Gazelle helicopters. Operational training for helicopter fliers is carried out at Portland on Lynx helicopters, at Yeovilton on the Commando Sea King, and of Culdrose preparing for specific roles, such as anti-submarine warfare, flying the Sea King Mk. 6.

A Flying Badge is awarded to those who successfully complete their initial training phases at Culdrose or RAF Cranwell, usually about ten months after the start of flying training. New pilot entrants can expect to reach operational status with the RN some 2½ years after joining the Service. Aircrew are not normally permitted to leave the Service until at least five years after the award of their Flying Badge.

The RN offers two types of commission for aircrew officers. A pensionable Medium Career Commission lasts 16 years or to the age of 38 years, whichever is the later. A Short Career Commission lasts 12 years, with an option to leave the Service after eight years with a tax-free gratuity but no pension.

Promotion within the RN is not tied to any particular stage in pilot training. A Midshipman entrant is promoted to Sub-Lieutenant (Acting or Confirmed status according to whether flying training has been completed or not) after two years' service. He should reach the rank of Lieutenant some five years after entry, although this can be reduced if seniority gains have been won during training. Graduates, who assume the rank of Acting Sub-Lieutenant, are confirmed in that rank on completion of operational flying training, unless they have already won promotion to Lieutenant in the meantime. There are opportunities for officers holding Short or Medium Career Commissions to convert these to Full Career Commissions within the four-to-nine years service period, although those who show outstanding ability may be given the opportunity to take a Full Career Commission earlier. Full Career transfer officers are automatically promoted to Lieutenant-Commander on achieving eight years', or, exceptionally, seven years' seniority. Promotion beyond the rank of Lieutenant-Commander is competitive, on merit.

The British Army

Unlike the RN and RAF, the Army employs non-commissioned officer (NCO) aircrew as well as officers. They are recruited from all regiments, arms and services of the Army, including the Army Air Corps (AAC). No soldier can enlist directly as aircrew because, before volunteering, they are required to have a proven soldierly track record and to have earned their Commanding Officer's recommendation. To this end they must have at least four years' service and have attained a minimum rank of Lance Corporal, with an unequivocal recommendation for promotion to Corporal. They are not required to have any certificated eduation qualifications, but they undergo the same tri-Service aptitude and medical tests as RAF fast-jet pilots and identical written and interview acceptance tests as serving Army officers. The latter include maths, military knowledge, basic engineering principles, map reading and signals. The selection board is looking for a bright, intelligent soldier, well experienced and versed in Army life and procedures and with the character and personality to live up to a demanding role. Although officers have previously passed a Regular Commission Board, they, too, go through exactly the same tests as the NCOs.

Having found the right personalities, they are then put through Flying Grading. This entails some 14 hours fixed-wing flying under very experienced instruction to see whether they can learn and retain flying skills and knowledge fast enough to get through the Army Pilot's Course. Those NCOs who pass the Grading Board are loaded on to Army Pilot's Courses, but serving officers have yet another hurdle to cross, as they are placed in order of merit for the limited number of vacancies. After that, both officers and NCOs go through the same pilot training.

The selection process is rigorous. Of those that pass through the first filter – their Commanding Officer's recommendation – some 30% fall by the wayside on aptitude, medical grounds or at the Selection Board. Of those that start Flying Grading, less than 50% are chosen. Even then, some 15 to 20% are unsuccessful on the Army Pilot's Course. Those who pass have most assuredly earned their wings.

NCO pilots come from two main sources, either from within the AAC or on secondment from other regiments or corps within the Army. Both are regarded without let or favour by the Selection Board. Non-AAC pilots may apply to transfer to the AAC one year after being awarded their wings, and about 70% of those who do are successful. Those who do not wish to, or are not selected for transfer, return to their parent arm after a three-year flying tour. Because they are not involved in the same staff and command structure, NCOs tend to build up more flying hours and pure flying experience than officers.

The AAC soldiers' careers start at the Army Training Regiment, Winchester, where they undergo the ten-week Common Military Syllabus (Recruits) Course. After this they move to the Army School of Mechanical Transport at Leaconfield for seven weeks, where they learn to drive large goods vehicles and Land Rovers. This is followed by three modules, each of three weeks, at the

School of Army Aviation at Middle Wallop, covering ground crewman skills, signals, aircraft refuelling and hazardous materials training. At the end of these courses the soliders are classified as a Groundcrewmen Class 3 and are ready to be posted to their first regiment.

The AAC accepts both male and female soldiers, and in 1995 11 female Airtroopers were serving in the Corps. They are expected to perform the same duties as their male counterparts and are treated equally with regard to career development.

There are two means of entry for Army officers; either as Direct Entry (DE) officers or by secondment from another regiment or corps in the Army. Opportunities for Direct Entry are as Regular Officers (Reg C) or Short Services Officers (SSC). Both types of commission are for a minimum of six years. The Reg C is to age 55, and the SSC may be extended to a maximum of eight years, depending upon the needs of the Army. SSC officers may apply for Reg C at the Royal Military Academy Sandhurst (RMAS) or during their service as qualified pilots. Entrants may be university graduates or accepted direct from school providing they have the minimum educational qualifications of five GCSE subjects at Grade C or equivalent (CSE 1) for SSC and two A levels for Reg C. Maths and English language must be included for both types of commission. Candidates with the minimum educational achievements are seldom considered unless they have other attributes, as competition for Direct Entry is fierce.

Age limits for DE commissions are 17¾ to 25 years at entry to RMAS. In practice few, if any, vacancies remain for DE AAC beyond the age of 22 for Reg C and 23 for SSC. It is therefore important that those attending university apply before graduation if they are to stand a good chance of selection. All DE candidates attend a two-day aircrew aptitude assessment and medical at RAF Cranwell, and a 3-week 14-hour Flying Grading Course at the School of Army Aviation (SAAvn) between the RCB and entrance to RMAS. Successful candidates continue to RMAS, while the others usually join another regiment of the army. Following a year in training at RMAS, all DE AAC officers spend six months commanding a platoon of soldiers in an infantry regiment or a troop of soldiers in a Royal Armoured Corps regiment before reporting to the SAAvn for their pilot course.

Officers from any regiment or corps in the Army may volunteer for secondment to the AAC after completing a minimum of two years' commissioned service, post-RMAS. Selection, which includes a quality assessment, follows the same format as DE candidates. The maximum age is 27 years, and the secondment is for an initial period of four years, including flying training. Successful candidates may then apply for a permanent transfer to the AAC one year after being awarded their wings, and many do achieve this. About 30% of officer pilots flying with the AAC are from other regiments. Applications to fly cannot be withheld.

Females may not join the AAC as DE officers. They may, however, be seconded to the AAC from other regiments or corps that accept females in the same way as male officers, and may transfer later in competition with their peers.

Candidates who successfully pass the Flying Grading Course are allocated a vacancy on the 42-week course that consists of three consecutive phases. The first phase involves two weeks of ground school followed by six weeks and 30 hours of elementary (fixed wing) flying to teach airmanship, precision and accuracy, the ability to recover from unusual attitudes and an introduction to instrument flying. Two further hours of ground school are included each day. Next comes one week of medical and survival training, followed by a further week of ground school before starting the second phase. This entails 14 weeks and 58 hours of basic (rotary-wing) flying, covering all the pure helicopter flying exercises. In phase three the student moves straight to operational flying training, divided into two parts. The first part, ten weeks, covers instrument flying, to achieve a non-procedural rating. It includes ultra-low-level manoeuvres using ground cover, observation and reconnaissance, artillery fire control, forward air control, advanced confined landing area landings, mountain flying, underslung-load work, long navigation exercises and internal security operations, together with many other military applications. The second part of phase three starts with two weeks of ground school and five weeks of helicopter tactical fieldcraft and tactical patrol work. The final week covers administration and the wings parade.

After 'wings', a proportion of the newly qualified pilots will convert to the Lynx. This involves seven weeks with 30 hours flying and 20 hours in a simulator, followed by two weeks of helicopter weapons training. The newly qualified pilots will join their operational units as the pilot in a crew of two; the other crew member is the Aircraft Commander. After achieving a minimum of six months and 350 flying hours, and having demonstrated the appropriate qualities, they will be eligible for appointment as Aircraft Commander as suitable vacancies occur. Depending on their role and additional duties, officers and NCO pilots with the AAC can expect to log between 600 and 1,000 flying hours during their three-year tour of duty.

In Civvy Street

What are the prospects for military pilots when they leave the Services? Overall they are very good, with demand for former service fliers by airlines and flying training establishments. Foreign governments, particularly those in the Middle East with friendly relations with Britain and British aircraft manufacturers, also place high value on former UK military personnel, and accordingly offer attractive short-term employment packages to those suitable qualified.

All three British armed forces demand minimum commitments of anything from six years upwards, which is entirely reasonable considering the immense cost of training. On leaving the Services, resettlement grants are payable which many ex-military pilots use to gain the civilian flying licences essential to obtain employment in the commercial field, no matter what military qualifications may be held. Professional flying schools (see Chapters 3 and 4) run specially-developed courses for ex-Service aircrew, who are usually permitted to count qualifying flight time logged in the forces towards an exemption from the full CPL course. The CAA will advise on specific requirements necessary in each individual case to gain the civilian licences or ratings.

Bear in mind, however, that as a reason for seeking a Service career, the prospect of subsequently getting a civilian flying job is unlikely to endear candidates to selection boards!

Chapter 6

Contact names and addresses

You are recommended to telephone before writing to any of the following addresses. Although they have all been individually checked at the time of going to press, the organisation may have moved or ceased to exist. Writing before checking may result in a long, agonising wait for a reply that is not going to come. In particular, with an application for employment or sponsorship, checking the address and correct name of an individual who will be dealing with your application is essential. Selection boards have been known to reject applications when it is evident that the candidate has not taken the time and trouble to check that the details are correct.

UK addresses have been listed by country or area. The Channel Islands, Isle of Man, Northern Ireland, Scotland and Wales have been listed alphabetically by area, as have the counties. Owing to recent and continuing boundary changes, each flying organisation has been listed under the county that they consider themselves in.

Although it is sometimes technically incorrect, this method should be easy and logical to use, as the reader will be looking for their own local area.

UK Private Pilot's Licence training schools and clubs – fixed-wing aircraft.

AVON

Bristol Flying Centre,
Bristol (Lulsgate) Airport,
Bristol, Avon BS19 3DT.
Telephone: 01275 474 601
Fax: 01275 474 851

Bristol & Wessex Aeroplane Club
Ltd., Bristol (Lulsgate) Airport,
Lulsgate, Bristol BS19 3EP.
Telephone: 01275 472 514
Fax: 01275 472 412

BEDFORDSHIRE

Bedfordshire School of Flying,
Cranfield Airfield,
Cranfield, Bedfordshire MK43 0JR
Telephone: 01234 752 817
Fax: 01234 750 395

Billins Air Services Ltd.,
Building 187, Cranfield Airfield,
Cranfield, Bedfordshire MK47 0AL.
Telephone: 01234 751 400
Fax: 01234 751 805

Bonus Aviation Ltd.,
Cranfield Airfield,
Cranfield, Bedfordshire. MK43 0JR.
Telephone: 01234 751 800
Fax: 01234 751 096

Cabair College of Air Training,
Cranfield Airfield,
Cranfield, Bedfordshire MK43 0JR.
Telephone: 01234 751 243
Fax: 01234 751 363

Eagle Flight Training,
The Ground Floor, Hangar 129,
Prince Way, London Luton Airport.
LU2 9PD
Telephone: 01582 720 007
Fax: 01582 435 130

Euroair,
Building 166, Cranfield Airport,
Cranfield, Bedfordshire MK43 0JR.
Telephone: 01234 752 262
Fax – as telephone

Henlow Flying Club,
c/o Henlow Camp,
Henlow, Bedfordshire SG16 3DN.
Telephone: 01462 851 936
Fax – as telephone

Skyline School of Flying Ltd
Fullers Hill Farm, Gransden,
Nr. Sandy, Bedfordshire SG19 3BP.
Telephone: 01767 651 950
Fax – as telephone

BERKSHIRE

West London Aero Club,
White Waltham Airfield,
Nr. Maidenhead, Berkshire SL6 3NJ.
Telephone: 01628 823 272
Fax: 01628 826 070

BUCKINGHAMSHIRE

British Airways Flying Club,
Wycombe Air Park, Booker,
Marlow, Buckinghamshire SL7 3DP.
Telephone: 01494 529 262
Fax: 01494 461 237

Denham School of Flying,
Denham Aerodrome, Denham,
Uxbridge, Middlesex UB9 5DE.
Telephone: 01895 833 327
Fax: 01895 835 048

The Pilot Centre Ltd.,
Denham Aerodrome,
Uxbridge, Middlesex UB9 5DF.
Telephone: 01895 833 838
Fax: 01895 832 267

Wycombe Air Centre Ltd.,
Wycombe Air Park, Booker,
Marlow, Buckinghamshire SL7 3DR.
Telephone: 01494 443 737
Fax: 01494 465 456

CAMBRIDGESHIRE

Cambridge Aero Club,
The Airport, New Market Road,
Cambridge CB5 8RX.
Telephone: 01223 373 214
Fax: 01223 373 833

Cambridge Flying Group,
The Airport, New Market Road,
Cambridge CB5 8RX.
Telephone: 01763 229 004
Fax: 01223 294 147

Klingair Flying Club (Klingair Ltd),
Peterborough Business Airfield,
Holme, Peterborough PE7 3PX.
Telephone: 01487 832 022
Fax: 01487 832 614

Rural Flying Corps,
Bourn Aerodrome, Cambridge,
Cambridgeshire CB3 7TQ.
Telephone: 01954 719 602
Fax – as telephone

Walkbury Flying Club,
Sibson Airfield, Wansford,
Peterborough,
Cambridgeshire CB3 7TQ.
Telephone: 01832 280 289
Fax – as telephone

CHANNEL ISLANDS

Channel Aviation Ltd.,
Planque Lane, Forest,
Guernsey, Channel Islands GY8 0DS.
Telephone: 01481 37217
Fax: 01481 38886

Guernsey Aero Club,
Planque Lane, Forest,
Guernsey, Channel Islands GY8 0DS.
Telephone: 01481 65254
Fax: 01481 63830

Jersey Aero Club,
States Airport, St Peter,
Jersey, Channel Islands JE3 7BP.
Telephone: 0153 443 990
Fax: 0153 441 290

CHESHIRE

Manchester School of Flying,
Business Aviation Centre Hangar 7,
Manchester Airport West,
Manchester M90 5NE
Telephone: 0161 436 0123
Fax: 0161 436 0125

CORNWALL

Cornwall Flying Club Ltd.,
Bodmin Airfield, Cardinham,
Bodmin, Cornwall PL30 4BU
Telephone: 0120 882 1419
Fax: 01208 821 711

Land's End Flying Club,
Land's End Aerodrome, St Just,
Penzance TR19 7RL.
Telephone: 01736 788 771
Fax: 01736 787 274

COUNTY DURHAM

Cleveland Flying School Ltd.,
Teesside International Airport,
Darlington, County Durham
DL2 1LU.
Telephone: 01325 332 855
Fax: 01325 332 043

St George Flying Club,
Teesside International Airport,
Darlington, County Durham
DL2 1RH.
Telephone: 01325 333 431
Fax – as telephone

Teesside Aero Club,
Teesside Airport, Darlington,
County Durham DL2 1LU.
Telephone: 01325 332 752
Fax: 01325 333 916

CUMBRIA

Border Air Training,
Hangar 30, Carlisle Airport,
Crosby on Eden,
Carlisle CA6 4NW.
Telephone: 01228 573 490
Fax: 01288 711 407

Carlisle Flight Centre,
Hangar 30, Carlisle Airport,
Crosby on Eden,
Carlisle CA6 4NW.
Telephone: 01228 573 333
Fax: 01288 573 311

Cumbria Aero Club,
Carlisle Airport,
Crosby on Eden,
Carlisle CA6 4NW.
Telephone: 01228 573 633
Fax – as telephone (voice contact first)

DERBYSHIRE

Derby Aero Club and Flying School,
Derby Airfield, Hilton Road,
Egginton, Derbyshire DE65 6GU.
Telephone: 01283 733 803
Fax: 01283 734 829

Donair Flying Club, Building 33,
Dakota Road, East Midlands Airport,
Castle Donington, Derby
DE74 2SA.
Telephone: 01332 810 444
Fax: 01332 812 726

East Midlands Flying School Ltd.,
Building 120, East Midlands Airport,
Castle Donington, Derby DE74 2SA.
Telephone: 01332 850 383
Fax: 01332 853 088

DEVON

Devon School of Flying,
Dunkeswell Aerodrome, Dunkeswell,
Nr. Honiton, Devon EX14 0RA.
Telephone: 01404 891 643
Fax: 01404 891 465

Eaglescott School of Flying,
Eaglescott Airfield, Burrington,
N. Devon EX37 9LJ.
Telephone: 0176 9520 404
Fax – not available

Exeter Air Training School Ltd.,
Building 12, Exeter Airport,
Exeter, Devon EX5 2BA.
Telephone: 01392 445 197
Fax – as telephone

Exeter Flying Club Ltd.,
Exeter Airport, Clyst Honiton,
Exeter, Devon EX5 2BA.
Telephone: 01392 367 653
Fax – as telephone (office hours)

Plymouth School of Flying Ltd.,
Plymouth City Airport, Crown Hill,
Plymouth, Devon PL6 8BW.
Telephone: 01752 773 335
Fax: 01752 770 252

DORSET

Airbourne School of Flying,
Hangar 406, Bournemouth Intl. Airport,
Christchurch, Dorset BH23 6NE.
Telephone: 01202 590 442
Fax: 01202 590 442

Cabair Training Group
(Bournemouth Flying School),
Building 198,
Bournemouth Intl. Airport,
Christchurch, Dorset BH23 6NE.
Telephone: 01202 578 558
Fax: 01202 570 203

Southern Flight Training Ltd.,
Building 66, South East Sector,
Bournemouth Intl. Airport
Christchurch, Dorset BH23 6SE.
Telephone: 01202 590 940
Fax: 01202 590 920

DURHAM – see entries under **COUNTY DURHAM**
EAST MIDLANDS – see entries under **DERBYSHIRE**

ESSEX

Andrewsfield Aviation Ltd.,
Saling Airfield, Great Dunmow,
Essex CM6 3TH.
Telephone: 01371 856 744
Fax: 01371 856 500

Aviator's Flight Centre,
Eastern Perimeter Road,
Southend Airport,
Southend-on-Sea, Essex SS2 6YF.
Telephone: 01702 542 497
Fax: 01702 511 390

Clacton Aero Club,
The Aerodrome, West Road,
Clacton-on-Sea, Essex CO15 1AG.
Telephone: 01255 424 671
Fax: 01255 475 364

Essex Flying Schools Ltd.,
c/o The Hangar, Earls Colne Airfield,
Earls Colne, Nr. Colchester, Essex
CO6 2NS.
Telephone: 01787 223 676
Fax: 01787 224 246

Seawing Flying Club Ltd.,
Eastern Perimeter Road, Southend
Airport,
Southend-on-Sea, Essex SS2 6YF.
Telephone: 01702 545 420
Fax – as telephone

Southend Flying Club,
Southend Airport, Cargo Entrance,
South Rd.
Southend-on-Sea, Essex SS2 6YF.
Telephone: 01702 545 198
Fax: 01702 543 756

Stapleford Flying Club,
Stapleford Aerodrome,
Nr. Romford, Essex RM4 1SJ.
Telephone: 01708 688 380
Fax: 01708 688 421

Willowair Flying Club,
London Southend Airport,
Southend-on-Sea, Essex SF2 6YT.
Telephone: 01702 531 555
Fax: 01702 542 070

GLOUCESTERSHIRE

Aeros Flying Club,
Building SE16,
Gloucestershire Airport,
Cheltenham, Gloucestershire
GL51 6SR.
Telephone: 01452 857 419
Fax: 01452 856 444

Archer Flight Training,
Building SE18, South East Area,
Cheltenham, Gloucestershire
GL51 6SR.
Telephone: 01452 713 830
Fax: 01452 857 021

Cotswold Aero Club,
Gloucestershire Airport, Staverton,
Gloucestershire GL51 6SP.
Telephone: 01452 713 924
Fax: 01452 854 122

Gloucester & Cheltenham School of
Flying,
Building SE4, Staverton Airport,
Cheltenham, Gloucestershire GL51 6SR.
Telephone: 01452 857 153
Fax – as telephone

Staverton Flying School,
Gloucestershire Airport,
Cheltenham, Gloucestershire
GL51 6ST.
Telephone: 01452 712 388
Fax: 01452 713 565

GREATER MANCHESTER – see entries under **CHESHIRE & LANCASHIRE**

HAMPSHIRE

Carill Aviation Flying School,
Building 2, Southampton Intl. Airport,
Southampton, Hampshire SO18 2NL.
Telephone: 01703 627 225
Fax: 01703 643 528

Solent Flight,
Building 2, Southampton Intl. Airport,
Southampton, Hampshire SO18 2NL.
Telephone: 01703 650 300
Fax: 01703 650 005

Western Air Training Ltd.,
Thruxton Airfield,
Andover, Hampshire SP11 8PW.
Telephone: 01264 773 900
Fax: 01264 773 913

HEREFORDSHIRE

Herefordshire Aero Club,
Shobdon Airfield, Leominster,
Herefordshire HR6 9NR.
Telephone: 01568 708 369
Fax: 01568 708 935

HERTFORDSHIRE

East Herts Flying School,
Panshanger Airfield, Cole Green,
Nr. Hertford, Hertfordshire SG14 2NH.
Telephone: 01707 391 791
Fax: 01707 392 792

Firecrest Aviation,
The Helicopter Hangar,
Elstree Aerodrome, Borehamwood,
Hertfordshire WD5 3AW.
Telephone: 0181 207 6201
Fax: 0181 207 4204

The London School of Flying,
Elstree Aerodrome, Borehamwood,
Hertfordshire WD6 3AW.
Telephone: 0181 953 4343
Fax: 0181 207 1509

Modern Air,
Fowlmere Aerodrome,
Royston, Hertfordshire SG8 7SJ.
Telephone: 01763 208 281
Fax: 01763 208 861

HUMBERSIDE – also see entries under **YORKSHIRE**

Frank Morgan School of Flying,
Humberside International Airport,
Kirmington, South Humberside.
DN39 6YH
Telephone: 01652 688 859
Fax: 01652 688 809

Humber Flying Club,
26 Franklin Way, Humberside Intl. Airport,
Kirmington, South Humberside
DN39 6YH.
Telephone: 01652 680 746
Fax: 01652 688 492

Humberside Flight Training Ltd.,
Plot 25, Schiphol Way, Humberside Intl. Airport.
Kirmington, South Humberside
DN39 6YH.
Telephone: 01652 688 056
Fax – as telephone

Triple 'A' Flying,
The Flight House, Kirmington Vale,
Barnetby, South Humberside
DN38 6AF.
Telephone: 01652 680 564
Fax: 01652 680 579

ISLE OF MAN

Ashley Gardner School of Flying,
55a Friary Park, Bellabeg,
Isle of Man IM9 4AW.
Telephone: 01624 823 454
Fax: 01624 825 744

Manx Flyers Aero Club,
The 27 Clubhouse, Derbyhaven,
Castletown, Isle of Man IM9 1TU.
Telephone: 01624 822 926
Fax – not available

KENT

Biggin Hill School of Flying,
Biggin Hill Airport, Biggin Hill,
Kent TN16 3BN.
Telephone: 01959 573 583
Fax: 01959 570 770

Civilair,
Building 174, Biggin Hill Aerodrome,
Biggin Hill, Kent TN16 3BN.
Telephone: 01959 573 853
Fax – as telephone

EFG Flying School,
Biggin Hill Aerodrome,
Biggin Hill, Kent TN16 3BN.
Telephone: 01959 540 400
Fax: 01959 576 857

Kingair Flight Centre,
Biggin Hill Aerodrome,
Biggin Hill, Kent TN16 3BN.
Telephone: 01959 575 088
Fax: 01959 572 163

Medway Flight Training,
(Farthing Corner Airfield)
Mattshill Road, Hartlip,
Nr. Sittingbourne, Kent ME9 7XA.
Telephone: 01634 389 757
Fax: 01634 264 011

Rochester Aviation Flying Club Ltd.,
Rochester Airport,
Chatham, Kent ME15 9SD.
Telephone: 01634 816 340
Fax – as telephone

Romney Marsh Aviation,
The Terminal Building,
Lydd, Kent TN29 9QL.
Telephone: 01797 320 734
Fax – as telephone

Surrey & Kent Flying Club,
Building 447, Biggin Hill Aerodrome,
Biggin Hill, Kent TN16 3BN
Telephone: 01959 572 255
Fax: 01959 571 357

Thanet Flying Club,
Manston Airport,
Ramsgate, Kent CT12 5BP.
Telephone: 01843 823 520
Fax: 01843 822 024

Weald Air Services Ltd.,
Headcorn Aerodrome,
Headcorn, Kent TN27 6NX.
Telephone: 01622 891 539
Fax: 01622 890 876

LANCASHIRE

Air Nova Flight Centre,
Building 9, Liverpool Airport North,
Liverpool L24 1YD.
Telephone: 0151 427 7907
Fax: 0151 427 7908

ANT Flying Club,
Blackpool Airport,
Squires Gate Lane, Blackpool FY4 2QS.
Telephone: 01253 343 102
Fax: 01253 345 396

Blackpool Air Centre,
Blackpool Airport,
Blackpool FY4 2QS
Telephone: 01253 341 871
Fax: 01253 341 567

Cheshire Air Training School,
Hangar 3, Liverpool Airport,
Liverpool L24 8QQ
Telephone: 0151 486 8383
Fax – as telephone

Comed Aviation Ltd.,
Blackpool Airport,
Blackpool FY4 2QY.
Telephone: 01253 349 072
Fax: 01253 349 073

The Lancashire Aero Club,
Barton Aerodrome, Liverpool Road,
Eccles M30 7SA.
Telephone: 0161 789 4785
Fax: 0161 787 8782

Liverpool Flying School Ltd.,
Hangar 4, Liverpool Airport North,
Liverpool L24 8QQ
Telephone: 0151 427 7449
Fax: 0151 427 0009

Ravenair, Business Aviation Centre,
South Terminal, Liverpool Airport,
Liverpool L24 1YD
Telephone: 0151 486 6161
Fax: 0151 486 5151

Westair Flying Services,
Squires Gate Lane,
Blackpool Airport, Blackpool FY4 2QX.
Telephone: 01253 404 925
Fax: 01253 401 121

LEICESTERSHIRE

Leicestershire Aero Club Ltd.,
Gartree Road,
Leicester LE2 2FG.
Telephone: 0116 2592 360
Fax: 0116 2592 712

LINCOLNSHIRE

Fenland Flying School,
Fenland Airfield, Holbeach St Johns,
Spalding, Lincolnshire PE12 8RQ.
Telephone: 01406 540 461
Fax – as telephone

Lincoln Aero Club,
Sturgate Airfield, Upton,
Gainsborough, Lincolnshire DN21 5PA.
Telephone: 01427 838 305 (week ends) 01522 721 411 (weekdays)
Fax: 01427 838 423

Lincoln Aviation
Wickenby Aerodrome, Langworth,
Lincolnshire LN3 5AA.
Telephone: 01673 885 886
Fax – as telephone

MERSEYSIDE – see entries under **LANCASHIRE**

MIDDLESEX

Denham School of Flying,
Denham Aerodrome, Uxbridge,
Middlesex UB9 5DE.
Telephone: 01895 833 327
Fax: 01895 835 048

The Pilot Centre,
Denham Aerodrome, Uxbridge,
Middlesex UB9 5DF.
Telephone: 01895 833 838
Fax: 01895 832 267

NORFOLK

The Norfolk County Flying Club Ltd.,
Unit 7c, Airport Business Centre,
Norwich Airport, Norwich NR6 6BS
Telephone: 01603 404 600
Fax: 01603 404 200

The Norwich School of Flying,
Liberator Road, Norwich Airport,
Norwich NR6 6EU.
Telephone: 01603 403 107
Fax: not available

NORTHAMPTONSHIRE

Airmaster Aviation Ltd,
Sywell Airport, Sywell
Northants NN6 0BN.
Telephone: 01604 645 691
Fax: 01604 645 996

Northamptonshire School of Flying Ltd.,
Sywell Airport, Sywell,
Northants NN6 0BN.
Telephone: 01604 644 678
Fax: 01604 495 324

Pilot Flight Training,
Hinton-in-the-Hedges Airfield, Steane,
Brackley, Northants NN13 5NS.
Telephone: 01295 812 775
Fax – as telephone

NORTHERN IRELAND

EAC Flight Training
Belfast International Airport,
Aldergrove,
Crumlin, County Antrim BT29 4AA
Telephone: 01849 422 789
Fax: 01849 452 649

Ulster Flying Club (1961) Ltd.,
Newtownards Airport,
PortaferryRoad,
County Down BT23 3SG.
Telephone: 01247 813 327
Fax: 01247 814 575

NORTHUMBERLAND – see entry under **TYNE & WEAR**

NOTTINGHAMSHIRE

ALH Skytrain,
Redford Gamston Airport,
Gamston, Nottinghamshire DN22 0QL
Telephone: 01777 838 202
Fax: 01777 838 035

Sheffield Aero Club,
Netherthorpe Airfield, Thorpe Salvin,
Nr. Worksop, Notts S80 3JQ
Telephone: 01909 475 233
Fax: 01909 532 413

The Sherwood Flying Club
(Nottingham Airport),
18 Ridge Lane, Radcliffe on Trent,
Nottingham NG12 1BD.
Telephone: 0115 9332 334
Fax: 0115 9332 442

OXFORDSHIRE

Enstone Flying Club,
Enstone Airfield, Churchenstone,
Oxfordshire OX7 4NP.
Telephone: 01608 678 204
Fax – as telephone

Oxford Air Training School,
Oxford Airport,
Kidlington, Oxford OX5 1RA.
Telephone: 01865 841 234
Fax: 01865 378 797

Pilot Flight Training,
Oxford Airport, Kidlington,
Oxford, Oxfordshire OX5 1RA.
Telephone: 01865 370 814
Fax – as telephone

SCOTLAND

Aberdeen Flying Club,
Wellheads Drive, Dyce,
Aberdeen AB2 0GQ.
Telephone: 01224 725 333
Fax: 01224 725 458

Edinburgh Flying Club,
Turnhouse Road,
Edinburgh EH12 0AL.
Telephone: 01313 394 990
Fax: 0131 339 7055

Far North Flight Training,
Wick Airport, Caithness,
Scotland KW1 4QP.
Telephone: 01955 602 201
Fax: 01955 602 203

Fife Flying Club,
Fife Airport,
Goatmilk,
Glenrothes, Fife, KY6 2SL
Telephone: 01592 753 792
Fax: 01592 612 812

Glasgow Flying Club,
132 Abbotsinch Road,
Paisley PA3 2RY.
Telephone: 0141 889 4565
Fax: 0141 840 2668

Highland Airways Ltd,
Inverness Airport,
Inverness IN1 2JB.
Telephone: 01667 462 664
Fax: 01667 462 696

Merlin Flying College,
Cumbernauld Airfield,
Duncan Mackintosh Rd.,
Cumbernauld G68 0HH.
Telephone: 01236 730 304
Fax: 01236 451 000

Prestwick Flight Centre,
179 North Side, Prestwick Airport,
Prestwick KA9 2SA.
Telephone: 0129 2476 523
Fax: 0129 2475 991

Tayside Aviation Ltd,
Perth Aerodrome,
Perth PE2 6NP
Telephone: 01738 553 357
Fax: 01738 553 369

Tayside Flying Club Ltd.,
Dundee Airport, Riverside Drive,
Dundee DD2 1UH.
Telephone: 01382 644 372
Fax: 01382 644 531

Turnhouse Flying Club,
Old Turnhouse Road,
Edinburgh EH12 9DN.
Telephone: 0131 339 4706
Fax: 0131 317 1429

SHROPSHIRE

Shropshire Aero Club Ltd.,
Sleap Aerodrome,
Harmer Hill, Shropshire SY4 3HE.
Telephone: 01939 232 882
Fax: 01939 235 058

STAFFORDSHIRE

East Staffordshire Flying Club,
Tatenhill Airfield, Newborough Road, Needwood,
Burton-on-Trent, Staffordshire DE13 9PD.
Telephone: 01283 575 283
Fax: 01283 575 650

SURREY

Blackbushe School of Flying,
Blackbushe Airport,
Nr. Camberley, Surrey GU17 9LQ.
Telephone: 01252 870 999
Fax: 01252 871 975

Cabair Flight Training Redhill,
The Control Tower,
Redhill, Surrey RH1 5YP.
Telephone: 01737 822 166
Fax: 01737 822 147

Cubair Flight Training Ltd,
Hangar 8, Kingsmill Lane,
Redhill Airfield, Redhill, Surrey
RH1 5YJ.
Telephone: 01737 822 124
Fax: 01737 822 115

European Flyers,
Blackbushe Airport,
Camberley, Surrey GU17 9LG.
Telephone: 01252 873 747
Fax: 01252 876 177

Fairoaks Flight Centre,
Fairoaks Airport,
Chobham, Surrey GU24 8HX.
Telephone: 01276 858 075
Fax: 01276 857 677

Redhill Aviation,
South Block, Redhill Aerodrome,
Kingsmill Lane, Surrey RH5 5JY.
Telephone: 01737 822 959
Fax: 01737 822 163

SUSSEX

Goodwood Flying School,
Goodwood Airfield, Goodwood,
Chichester, Sussex PO18 0PH.
Telephone: 01243 755 066
Fax: 01243 755 065

Sky Leisure Aviation,
Main Terminal Building,
Shoreham Airport,
Shoreham by Sea, West Sussex
BN43 5FF.
Telephone: 01273 464 422
Fax – as telephone

Southernair Ltd.,
Shoreham Airport,
Shoreham by Sea, West Sussex
BN43 5FF.
Telephone: 01273 461 661
Fax: 01273 454 020

Sussex Flying Club Ltd.,
First Floor, Terminal Building,
Shoreham Airport, West Sussex
BN43 5FF.
Telephone: 01273 440 852
Fax – as telephone

Vectair Aviation,
Goodwood Airfield, Goodwood,
Chichester, Sussex PO18 0PH
Telephone: 01243 781 652
Fax: 01243 771 322

TEESSIDE – see entries under **COUNTY DURHAM**

TYNE & WEAR

Newcastle Aero Club Flying School,
Woolvington, Newcastle-upon-Tyne
NE13 8BT.
Telephone: 0191 286 1321
Fax – as telephone

WALES

Air Caernarfon Flying Club,
Caernarfon Airport, Dinasdinlle,
Gwynedd LL54 5TP.
Telephone: 01286 830 475
Fax: 01286 830 280

Cardiff Aeronautical Services Ltd.,
The White House,
Cardiff-Wales Intl. Airport,
Rhoose, South Glamorgan CF62 3BD
Telephone: 01446 711 987
Fax – as telephone (voice contact first)

Cardiff-Wales Flying Club,
The White Building,
Cardiff-Wales Airport,
Rhoose, South Glamorgan
CF62 3BD.
Telephone: 01446 710 000
Fax: 01446 710 535

Haverfordwest School of Flying,
Haverfordwest Aerodrome,
Haverfordwest, Dyfed SA62 4BN.
Telephone: 01437 760 822
Fax – as telephone

Mona Flying Club,
RAF Mona, Gwalchmi, Gwynedd,
Isle of Anglesey LL65 3NY.
Telephone: 01407 720 581 (no fax)
Ops. winter weekends/summer evenings and weekends

Swansea Aero Club & Flying School,
Swansea Airport, Fairwood Common,
Swansea SA2 7JU.
Telephone: 01792 204 063
Fax: 01792 297 923

Welshpool Flying School,
Mid-Wales Airport,
Welshpool, Powys SY21 8SG.
Telephone: 01938 555 062
Fax: 01938 555 487

WARWICKSHIRE

Avon Flying School Ltd.,
Wellesbourne Airfield, Wellesbourne,
Warwickshire CV35 9EU.
Telephone: 01789 470 727
Fax – as telephone

Coventry Flying School,
Rowley Road,
Nr. Coventry CV3 4FR.
Telephone: 01203 301 428
Fax: 01203 306 417

Midland Air Training School,
Coventry Air Park, Coventry Airport,
Coventry CV3 4FR.
Telephone: 01203 304 914
Fax – not available

RS Pilot Training,
Wellesbourne Airfield, Wellesbourne,
Warwickshire CV35 9EU.
Telephone: 01789 470 434
Fax – as telephone

South Warwickshire Flying School,
Wellesbourne Mountford Airfield,
Warwick, Warwickshire CV35 9EU.
Telephone: 01789 840 094
Fax: 01789 842 593

Wellesbourne Aviation Ltd.,
Wellesbourne Mountford Airfield,
Warwick, Warwickshire CV35 9EU.
Telephone: 01789 841 066
Fax: 01789 841 07

WEST MIDLANDS

Ace Air Training, Building 29b,
Halfpenny Green Airfield, Bobbington,
Nr. Stourbridge, West Midlands
DY7 5DY.
Telephone: 01384 221 292
Fax: not available

Halfpenny Green Flight Centre Ltd.,
Halfpenny Green Airport,
Bobbington, Nr. Stourbridge,
West Midlands DY7 5DY.
Telephone: 01384 221 456
Fax: 01384 221 006

Midland Flight Centre,
Halfpenny Green Airport, Bobbington,
Nr. Stourbridge, West Midlands
DY7 5DY.
Telephone: 01384 221 011
Fax – as telephone

Warwickshire Aerocentre Ltd.,
Old Firewatch Building,
Hangar Road, Birmingham Airport
(Cargo) B26 3QN.
Telephone: 0121 782 1011
Fax: 0121 782 4256

WILTSHIRE

Abbas Air,
Compton Abbas Airfield, Ashmore,
Salisbury, Wiltshire SP5 5AP.
Telephone: 01747 811 767
Fax: 01747 811 161

Old Sarum Flying Club,
Hangar 3, Portway,
Salisbury, Wiltshire SP4 6DJ.
Telephone: 01722 322 525
Fax: 01722 323 702

Wessex Aero Club,
3 Mendip View Cottages,
Clutton Hill, Clutton, Bristol BS18 4QQ.
Telephone: 01761 452 991
Fax: 01761 453 306

YORKSHIRE – also see entries under **HUMBERSIDE**

Full Sutton Flight Centre Ltd.,
Full Sutton Airfield, Stamford Bridge,
York, Yorkshire YO4 1HS.
Telephone: 01759 372 717
Fax: 01759 372 991

Old and new. The RAF's long-serving Jet Provost T.5A basic trainers (background) are being replaced by Shorts Tucano T.1 turboprops such as this one from No.1 FTS at RAF Linton-on-Ouse. (Peter R. March)

After basic training, RAF pilots fly BAe Hawk T.1/1As for advanced and weapons training. (British Aerospace)

Where every would-be RAF pilot imagines himself one day: flying a Tornado F.3, the service's principal air defence fighter. (Mike Jerram)

British Aerospace/McDonnell Douglas Harrier GR.5/7s are replacing the earlier Harrier GR.3 (background) with RAF V/STOL squadrons. This GR.5 one is from 20 Squadron Operational Conversion Unit based at RAF Wittering, Cambridgeshire. (Ministry of Defence)

Boeing Vertol Chinook H.C.I. is the RAF's heavy lift helicopter.
(Boeing Helicopter Company)

Multi-engine training for RAF pilots is conducted on British Aerospace Jetstream twin turboprops from RAF Leeming in Yorkshire.

British Aerospace Nimrod MR.2 maritime reconnaissance aircraft. (Mike Jerram)

Westland Gazelle helicopter lifting off for a training sortie at the Army Air Corps Centre, Middle Wallop. (Mike Jerram)

Hull Aero Club,
Lindley Hill Airfield,
Lindley Hill Road,
Leven, Beverley, North Humberside
HU17 9LT.
Telephone: 01964 544 994
Fax – as telephone

Multiflight Ltd.,
Leeds-Bradford Airport,
Yeadon, Leeds LS19 7YG.
Telephone: 0113 2391 339
Fax: 0113 2391 326

Imperial Aviation (Sandtoft) Ltd.,
Sandtoft Aerodrome, Belton,
Nr Epworth, Doncaster DN9 1PN.
Telephone: 01427 873 676
Fax: 01427 874 656

Sherburn Aero Club,
The Airfield, Lennerton Lane,
Sherburn-in-Elmet, Nr. Leeds
LS25 6JE.
Telephone: 01977 682 674
Fax: 01977 683 699

Yorkshire Aeroplane Club,
Leeds–Bradford Airport,
Yeadon, Nr. Leeds LS19 7TU.
Telephone: 0113 2503 840
Fax: 0113 2500 464

UK Private Pilot's Licence training schools and clubs – helicopters.

BUCKINGHAMSHIRE
Virgin Helicopters Ltd,
Wycombe Air Park, Nr. Marlow,
Buckinghamshire SL7 3DR
Telephone: 01494 538 887
Fax: 01494 450 627

ESSEX
Direct Helicopters,
London Southend Airport,
Southend-on-Sea, Essex SS2 6YP.
Telephone: 01702 546 420
Fax: 01702 542 104

HAMPSHIRE
FAST Helicopters Ltd.,
Thruxton Airfield,
Andover, Hampshire SP11 8PW.
Telephone: 01264 772 508
Fax: 01264 773 824

KENT
Thurston Helicopters,
The Aerodrome, Headcorn,
Kent TN27 9HX.
Telephone: 01622 891 158
Fax: 01622 891 814

LANCASHIRE
Helicentre Ltd.,
Blackpool Airport, Squires Gate Lane,
Blackpool FY4 2QY.
Telephone: 01253 343 082
Fax: 01253 407 351

LANCASHIRE
The Manchester Helicopter Centre,
Barton Airport, Eccles,
Manchester M30 7SA.
Telephone: 0161 787 7125
Fax: 0161 787 7892

LEICESTERSHIRE
East Midlands Helicopters,
Oaklands, Loughborough Road,
Loughborough, Leicestershire
LE12 6RQ.
Telephone: 01509 856 464
Fax: 01509 856 444

MIDDLESEX
Helair Ltd.,
Denham Aerodrome,
Uxbridge, Middlesex UB9 5DF.
Telephone: 01895 835 899
Fax: 01895 835 838

NORFOLK
Sterling Helicopters Ltd.,
Hangar 6, Javelin Road,
Norwich NR6 6HX.
Telephone: 01603 417 156
Fax: 01603 410 791

NORTHAMPTONSHIRE
CJ Helicopters (Sywell),
15 Marlowe Close, East Hunsbury,
Northamptonshire NN4 0QQ.
Telephone: 01604 760 760
Fax: 01604 702 902

NORTHAMPTONSHIRE
Sloane Helicopters Ltd.,
The Business Aviation Centre Sywell,
Northampton NN6 0BN.
Telephone: 01604 790 595
Fax: 01604 790 988

NORTHERN IRELAND
Helicopter Training & Hire Ltd.,
General Aviation Building,
Belfast Intl. Airport, Belfast,
BT29 4JT
Telephone: 01849 453663
Fax: 01849 423 233

SURREY
Alan Mann Helicopters Ltd.,
Fairoaks Airport, Chobham,
Nr Woking, Surrey GU24 8HX.
Telephone: 01276 857 471
Fax: 01276 857 037.

SURREY
Cabair Flight Training Redhill,
The Control Tower,
Redhill, Surrey RH1 5YP.
Telephone: 01737 822 166
Fax: 01737 822 147

SURREY
Redhill Helicopter Centre,
Hangar 1, Redhill Aerodrome,
Redhill, Surrey RH1 5YP.
Telephone: 01737 823 282
Fax: 01737 823 118

SURREY
Thurston Helicopters,
Redhill Aerodrome,
Redhill, Surrey RH1 5JY.
Telephone: 01737 823 514
Fax: 01737 822 683

SUSSEX
Southernair Ltd.,
Shoreham Airport,
Shoreham by Sea, West Sussex
BN43 5FF.
Telephone: 01273 461 661
Fax: 01273 454 020

WARWICKSHIRE
Heliair Ltd.,
Wellesbourne Airfield,
Nr. Warwick,
Warwickshire CV35 9EU.
Telephone: 01789 470 476
Fax: 01789 470 466

YORKSHIRE
Heliscott Flight Training,
Walton Wood Airfield, Thorpe Audlin,
Pontefract, West Yorkshire WF8 3HQ.
Telephone: 01977 621 378
Fax: 01977 620 868

YORKSHIRE
Helijet Aviation
Leeds Heliport, Leeds, LS19 7XS.
Telephone: 0113 2500 588
Fax: 0113 2508 161

YORKSHIRE
Yorkshire Helicopter Centre,
6 Swinton Meadows,
Mexborough, S. Yorkshire S64 8AB.
Telephone: 01709 571 720
Fax: 01709 571 721

Non-UK Private Pilot's Licence training schools and clubs – fixed wing.

The organisations marked √ have stated that they are able to instruct in line with the UK CAA syllabus. Potential students are strongly recommended to satisfy themselves as to the full details of any flying course and ground school exams before committing to training. The other schools listed instruct in line with their own country's aviation authority's rules.

The following only include, where possible, foreign schools who offer a UK contact telephone number or a USA direct UK **Free***fone* number. For countries where such schools do not seem to exist, those that advertise in the UK, and appear keen to encourage UK students, have been listed.

AUSTRALIA
Rossair Flying Centre,
Parafield Airport, Kittyhawke Lane,
Adelaide, South Australia.
Telephone: 00 618 8258 2211
Fax: 00 618 8281 4430

CANADA
Moncton Flight Centre,
PO Box 250, Dept. 136, Moncton,
Canada E1C 8K9.
Telephone: UK Agent (R. Heald)
01392 221 366
Fax: UK Agent 01392 495 953

FRANCE
Languedoc Aviation Carcassonne, √
Salvaza Airport, Carcassonne,
Rousillon, France.
Telephone: UK Agent (M. Evans)
0181 946 6950
Fax: UK Agent 01959 540 079

CYPRUS
Griffon Aviation (Cyprus) Ltd.,
13 Eric Mendelson, PO Box 6121,
3304 Limassol, Cyprus.
Telephone: 00357 6422 350
Fax: 00357 6422 360

CANADA
Nelson Mountain Air,
Lakeside Group, Box 9, Nelson,
British Columbia V1L 6B9.
Telephone & Fax:
UK Agent (Ian Clacher) 01305 852 525

CYPRUS
Tomahawk Aviation Ltd., √
PO Box 2614, Larnaca,
Cyprus.
Telephone: 00357 4625 033
Fax: 00357 4625 341

FRANCE
Sisteron Valley Flying Club, √
Aerodrome Sisteron, Thèze,
Vaumeilh, 04200 France.
Telephone: UK Agent (R. Brooks)
0171 724 8380
Fax: UK Agent 0171 258 1466

IRELAND
Euro Aer Training,
Waterford Airport, Killowen,
Waterford, Ireland.
Telephone: 003 535 152 636
Fax: 003 535 152 637

IRELAND
Sligo Aero Club,
Sligo Airport, Strandhill,
Sligo, Ireland.
Telephone: 003 537 168 280
(ask for aero club)
Fax: 003 537 168 396

KENYA
Kenya School of Flying,
PO Box 74714,
Nairobi, East Africa.
Telephone: 002 542 500 374
Fax: 002 542 503 651

NEW ZEALAND
Air Academy Hastings,
Bridge Pa Aerodrome, PO Box 2199,
Hastings, New Zealand.
Telephone: 00 646 879 8466
Fax: 00 646 879 9805

SOUTH AFRICA
43 Air School,
Private Bag X43,
Port Alfred 6170.
Telephone: UK Agent 01568 610 546
Fax: UK Agent 01568 614 361

SOUTH AFRICA
Progress Flight Academy,
PO Box 28,
Greenbushes 6390, South Africa.
Telephone: 002 741 721 647
Fax: 002 741 722 061

UNITED STATES
Air Desert Pacific,
1889 McKinley Avenue, La Verne.
California 91750, USA.
Telephone: UK Agent (Neil
Wollacott) 01271 45425
Fax: (USA) 001 909 596 9852

UNITED STATES
Aviator Inc.,
PO Box 79, Addison Airport,
Dallas, Texas 75001, USA.
Telephone: UK Agent (Successair)
01704 876 553
Fax: (USA) 001 214 702 8383

UNITED STATES
Avtar Inc.,
PO Box 526628, Miami,
Florida 33152–6628, USA.
Telephone: UK Agent (D. Deighton)
01376 584 964
Fax: UK Agent 01376 583 976

UNITED STATES
Cecily's Flight Center, √
Albert Whitted Airport,
St Petersburg, Florida 33701, USA.
Telephone: UK Agent (D. Kipling)
01702 526 292
Fax: UK Agent 01702 511 390

UNITED STATES
Crystal Aero Group Inc.,
PO Box 2050, Crystal River,
Florida 34423, USA.
Telephone: UK Agent (B. Sperring)
01872 261 126
Fax: (USA) 001 904 795 1730

UNITED STATES
Everything Flyable Inc.,
3333 East Spring Street, 3rd Floor,
Long Beach, California 90806, USA.
Telephone: UK Agent (Gary Moore)
0139 2877 660
Fax: (USA) 001 310 989 3134

UNITED STATES
Firefox Aviation Inc.,
12017 Bells Ferry Road,
Canton, Georgia 30114, USA.
Telephone: 0800 962 080 (**Free***fone*)
Fax: (USA) 001 404 720 7796

UNITED STATES
Ormond Beach Aviation, √
770 Airport Road, Ormond Beach,
Florida 32174, USA.
Telephone: 0800 892 133 (**Free***fone*)
Fax: (USA) 001 904 673 0379

UNITED STATES
San Diego Flight Training International,
Montgomery Field, 8745 Aero Drive,
Ste 103, San Diego, California 92123, USA.
Telephone: UK Agent 01344 485 638
Fax: (USA) 001 619 569 5030

UNITED STATES
Southeastern School of Aeronautics,
Herbert Smart Downtown Airport,
Macon, Georgia 31201, USA.
Telephone: 0800 895 083 (**Free***fone*)
Fax: (USA) 001 912 742 8022

The Aircraft Owners and Pilot's Association contact numbers and addresses for each of the above countries are listed on page 137.

Non-UK Private Pilot's Licence training schools and clubs – helicopters.

CYPRUS
Helimed Ltd.,
Paphos International Airport,
Paphos, Cyprus.
Telephone: 003 576 422 840
Fax: 003 576 422 756

FRANCE
Sisteron Valley Flying Club, √
Aerodrome Sisteron, Thèze,
Vaumeilh, 04200 France.
Telephone: UK Agent (R. Brooks) 0171 724 8380
Fax: UK Agent 0171 258 1466

IRELAND
Helifly Ireland (Galway) Ltd.,
Town Park Centre,
Tuam Road, Galway, Ireland.
Telephone: 003 5391 752 572
Fax: 003 5391 752 870

NEW ZEALAND
Heli-flight Wairarapa Ltd.,
31 High Street, Masterton,
New Zealand.
Telephone: 006 463 771 104
Fax – as telephone

UNITED STATES
Helicopter Adventures Inc.,
81 John Glenn Drive, Concord,
California 94520, USA.
Telephone: UK Agent (M. Beeley) 0181 8788 615
Fax: (USA) 001 510 686 2986

UNITED STATES
International Helicopter Academy Inc.,
1585 Aviation Center Parkway,
PO Box 10437,
Daytona Beach, Florida 32120, USA.
Telephone: 0800 961 579 (**Free***fone*)
Fax: (USA) 001 904 253 1991

The Aircraft Owners and Pilot's Association contact numbers and addresses for each of the above countries are listed on page 137.

Professional Pilot flight training schools – UK

Bristow Helicopters,
Redhill Aerodrome,
Redhill, Surrey RH1 5JZ.
Telephone: 01737 822 353
Fax: 01737 822 694

British Aerospace Flying Training (UK) Ltd, Prestwick Airport,
Ayrshire, Scotland KA9 2RW.
Telephone: 01292 671 022
Fax: 01292 474 016

Cabair College of Air Training,
Cranfield Aerodrome,
Cranfield, Bedford, Bedfordshire MK43 0JR.
Telephone: 01234 751 243
Fax: 01234 751 363

London Guildhall University,**
100 The Minories,
London EC3N 1JY.
Telephone: 0171 320 1000
Fax: 0171 320 1759

Oxford Air Training School,
Oxford Airport, Kidlington,
Oxfordshire OX5 1RA.
Telephone: 01865 841 234
Fax: 01865 841 795

Professional Pilot Study Centre,**
Bournemouth International Airport,
Christchurch, Dorset BH23 6DN.
Telephone: 01202 579 819
Fax: 01202 580 150

**Ground tuition only. These establishments do not offer flying training.

The above list is current as at August 1998. They are updated monthly, as required, by the CAA. For a current list contact the Civil Aviation Authority (FCL3) Aviation House, South Area, Gatwick Airport, West Sussex RH6 0YR, or telephone: 01293 573 700.

British airlines, scheduled, charter and cargo operators

Air 2000 First Choice House, London Road, Crawley, West Sussex RH10 2GX.
Telephone: 01293 518 966 Fax: 01293 588 757

Air Bristol Bristol Filton Airport, PO Box 92, Patchway, Bristol, Avon BS12 7YA.
Telephone: 0117 936 4932 Fax: 0117 936 4932

Air Atlantique Hangar 5, Coventry Airport, Warwickshire CV8 3AZ.
Telephone: 01203 307 566 Fax: 01203 307 703

Air Foyle Halcyon House, Luton Airport, Bedfordshire LU2 9LU.
Telephone: 01582 420 100 Fax: 01582 400 958

Air Kilroe Hangar 6, North Road, Manchester International Airport, Manchester M90 1PF.
Telephone: 0161 436 2055 Fax: 0161 499 1890

Airtours International Parkway Three, 300 Princess Road, Manchester M14 7LU.
Telephone: 0161 232 6600 Fax: 0161 232 6610

Air UK Stansted House, London–Stansted Airport, Essex CM24 8QT.
Telephone: 01279 660 400 Fax: 01279 660 111

Air UK Leisure Airways House, London–Stansted Airport, Stansted, Essex CM24 1RY.
Telephone: 01279 680 737 Fax: 01279 680 172

Atlantic Air Transport/Atlantic Airways/Atlantic Cargo – see entry under **Air Atlantique**

Aurigny Air Services The Airport, Alderney, Channel Islands.
Telephone: 01481 822 886 Fax: 01481 823 344

BAC Express Airlines BAC House, Bonehurst Road, Horley, Surrey RH6 8QG.
Telephone: 01293 821 621 Fax: 01293 821 204

Bond Air Services Aberdeen Airport, Dyce, Aberdeen AB2 0DU.
Telephone: 01224 725 505 Fax: 01224 722 425

Bristow Helicopters Redhill Aerodrome, Redhill, Surrey RH1 5JZ.
Telephone: 01737 822 353 Fax: 01737 822 694

Britannia Airways Luton Airport, Bedfordshire LU2 9ND.
Telephone: 01582 424 155 Fax: 01582 458 594

British Air Ferries – see entry under **British World Airlines**

British Airways Speedbird House, London–Heathrow Airport, Middlesex TW6 2JA.
Telephone: 0181 759 5511 Fax: 0181 564 1452

British International Helicopters Aberdeen Airport, Buchan Road, Dyce, Aberdeen AB2 0DT.
Telephone: 01224 771 353 Fax: 01224 771 632

British Midland Donington Hall, Castle Donington, Derbyshire DE7 2SB.
Telephone: 01332 810 741 Fax: 01334 854 314

British World Airlines Viscount House, Southend Airport, Southend-on-Sea, Essex SS2 6YL.
Telephone: 01702 354 435 Fax: 01702 331 914

Brymon Airways Plymouth City Airport, Crownhill, Plymouth, Devon PL6 8TP.
Telephone: 01752 705 151 Fax: 01752 795 590

Business Air Kirkhill Business House, Howemoss Drive, Dyce, Aberdeen AB2 0GL.
Telephone: 01224 725 566 Fax: 01224 770 141

Caledonian Airways Caledonian House, Gatwick Airport, West Sussex RH6 0LF.
Telephone: 01293 536 321 Fax: 01293 668 353

Channel Express Air Services Building 470, Bournemouth Intl. Airport, Christchurch, Dorset BH23 6DL.
Telephone: 01202 570 701 Fax: 01202 577 628

Cityflyers Express Iain Stewart Centre, Beehive Ring Road, Gatwick Airport, West Sussex RH6 0PB.
Telephone: 01293 567 837 Fax: 01293 567 829

DHL Air East Midlands Airport, Castle Donington, Derby DE7 2SB.
Telephone: 01332 850 666 Fax: 01332 850 651

FlightLine Aviation Way, Southend Airport, Southend-on-Sea, Essex SS2 6UN.
Telephone: 01702 543 000 Fax: 01702 547 778

FR Aviation Bournemouth International Airport, Christchurch, Dorset BH23 6DL.
Telephone: 01202 409 000 Fax: 01202 580 936

GB Airways Iain Stewart Centre, Beehive Ring Road, Gatwick Airport, West Sussex RH6 0PB.
Telephone: 01293 664 239 Fax: 01293 664 218

Heavylift Cargo Airlines London–Stansted Airport, Stansted, Essex CM24 8QP.
Telephone: 01279 680 611 Fax: 01279 680 615

Hunting Cargo Airlines East Midlands Airport, Castle Donington, Derbyshire DE74 2SA.
Telephone: 01332 810 081 Fax: 01332 811 491

Instone Air Services Charity Farm, Pulborough Rd., Paraham, Pulborough, W. Sussex RH20 4HP.
Telephone: 01903 740 101 Fax: 01903 740 102

Jersey European Airways Terminal Building, Exeter Airport, Clyst Honiton, Devon EX5 2BD.
Telephone: 01392 366 669 Fax: 01392 366 151

Knight Air Leeds–Bradford Airport, Yeadon, Leeds, West Yorkshire LS19 7YG.
Telephone: 01132 391 339 Fax: 01132 391 326

Loganair St Andrews Drive, Glasgow Airport, Paisley, Scotland PA3 2TG.
Telephone: 0141 889 1311 Fax: 0141 887 6020

Maersk Air Ltd Maersk Air House, 2245–2249, Coventry Road, Birmingham B26 3NG.
Telephone: 0121 743 9090 Fax: 0121 743 4123

MK Airlines Landhurst, Hartfield, East Sussex TN7 4DL.
Telephone: 01892 770 011 Fax: 01892 770 022

Monarch Airlines Luton International Airport, Bedfordshire LU2 9NU.
Telephone: 01582 424 211 Fax: 01582 411 000

Sabre Airways 12 The Merlin Centre, County Oak Way, Crawley, West Sussex RH11 7XA.
Telephone: 01293 410 727 Fax: 01293 410 737

Sky Air Cargo Unit 2, Mapleking House, 55/57, Park Royal Road, London NW10 7JH.
Telephone: 0181 961 0932 Fax: 0181 961 0956

Suckling Airways Cambridge Airport, Cambridge CB5 8RT.
Telephone: 01223 292 525 Fax reserved for passenger bookings only

Titan Airways Enterprise House, Stansted Airport, Stansted, Essex CM24 1QW.
Telephone: 01279 680 616 Fax: 01279 680 110

TNT International Aviation Archway House, 114–116 St Leonards Road, Windsor, Berkshire SL4 3DG.
Telephone: 01753 842 168 Fax: 01753 858 172

Virgin Atlantic Airways Virgin Flight Centre, Unit 1A, Old Brighton Road, Lowfield Heath, Crawley, West Sussex RH11 0PR.
Telephone: 01293 562 345 Fax: 01293 747 880

Contact addresses – private, commercial and airline pilots – non-U.K.

Aircraft Owners & Pilots Association (Australia)
38 Fyshwick Plaza, 59 Wollongong Street, PO Box 1065, Fyshwick, ACT 2609, Australia.
Telephone: 0061 280 4221 Fax: 0061 280 7341

Aircraft Owners & Pilots Association (Canada)
PO Box 734, Ottawa, Ontario, Canada K1P 5S4.
Telephone: 001 613 236 4901 Fax: 001 613 236 8646

Aircraft Owners & Pilots Association (Cyprus)
PO Box 1890, Nicosia, Cyprus
Dr. Nicolas E Aristodemou.
Telephone: 00357 2466 842 or 00357 2450 402 Fax: 00357 2453 661

Aircraft Owners & Pilots Association (France)
Batiment Paul-Bert, Bereau No. 25 F-93350, Aéroport le Bourget, France.
Telephone: 0033 4835 9294 Fax: 0033 4835 9640

Aircraft Owners & Pilots Association (Ireland)
Loughlinstown Road, Celbridge, Co Kildare, Ireland.
Telephone: 0035 317 001 826 Fax: 0035 314 571 509

Aircraft Owners & Pilots Association (UK)
50a Cambridge Street, London SW1V 4QQ.
Telephone: 0171 834 5631 Fax: 0171 834 8623

Aircraft Owners & Pilots Association (New Zealand)
Hoskyns Road, West Melton, RD5, Christchurch, New Zealand.
Telephone: 00 643 358 7573 Fax: 00 643 358 4150

Aircraft Owners & Pilots Association (South Africa)
PO Box 6666, Pretoria 0001, Republic of South Africa.
Telephone: 00 2712 787 0520 Fax: 00 2712 789 1512

Aircraft Owners & Pilots Association (United States)
421 Aviation Way, Frederick, Maryland 21701, USA
Telephone: 001 301 695 2000 Fax: 001 301 695 2375

Aviation Training Association
125 London Road, High Wycombe, Buckinghamshire HP11 1BT.
Telephone: 01494 445 262 Fax: 01494 439 984

British Air Line Pilots Association
81 New Road, Harlington, Hayes, Middlesex GB3 5BG.
Telephone: 0181 476 4000 Fax: 0181 476 4077

British Helicopter Advisory Board
The Graham Suite, West Entrance, Fairoaks Airport, Chobham, Surrey GU24 8HX.
Telephone: 01276 856 100 Fax: 01276 856 126

Civil Aviation Authority (flight crew licencing)
Aviation House, South Area, Gatwick Airport, West Sussex RH6 0YR.
Telephone: (Touch-tone phone menu for departments, or hold for a human) 01293 567 171 Fax: (all FCL departments) 01293 573 996

Civil Aviation Authority (general enquiries)
Aviation House, South Area, Gatwick Airport, West Sussex RH6 0YR.
Telephone: (main switchboard) 01293 567 171 Fax: departments have individual faxes

Federal Aviation Administration Office
US Embassy, 5 Upper Grosvenor Street, London W1A 2JB.
Telephone: 0171 499 9000 Fax: 0171 491 1128

Federal Aviation Administration Unit
Aviation House, South Area, Gatwick Airport, West Sussex RH6 0YR.
No telephone – Please use fax on 01293 573 992, or write to the above address

Guild of Air Pilots & Air Navigators
Cobham House, 291 Grays Inn Road, London WC1X 8QF.
Telephone: 0171 837 3323 Fax: 0181 953 5219

PPL/IR Network
Peter Herold, Flat 2, Windsor Court, The Pavement, London SW4 0JF.
Telephone: 0171 720 9382 Fax: 0171 652 2115

Student Pilot's Association
30 Tisbury Road, Hove, East Sussex BN3 3BA.
Telephone: 01273 204 080 Fax – not available

Contact numbers and addresses – military

British Army
The British Army is unique among the Services in offering pilot careers to non-commissioned officers as well as officers. It does not, however, like the RAF and RN, recruit pilots directly from civilian life, but recruits from all regiments, arms and services of the Army, including the Army Air Corps. For further details see page 109.

Royal Air Force

If you require more details of an RAF career, contact your nearest RAF Careers Information Office from the following list. At the time of writing, the existence of many of these offices is under review. If the number is unobtainable, write or telephone:

Director of Recruitment Selection,
Officer and Aircrew Selection Centre,
RAF Cranwell, Sleaford, Lincolnshire NG34 8HB.
Telephone: (Main switchboard) 01400 261 201
Fax: (Officer and Aircrew Selection Centre) 01400 262 220, extension 6736

Town	Telephone
Aberdeen	01224 640 251
Birmingham	01216 436 289
Bournemouth	01202 554 085
Brighton	01273 327 428
Bristol	0117 9294 051
Cardiff	01222 227 626
Chatham	01634 845 285
Exeter	0139 254 204
Glasgow	01412 214 852
Gloucester	01452 524 538
Inverness	01463 235 610
Leeds	01132 432 914
Leicester	01162 624 940
Liverpool	01512 361 566
London	0171 636 0782
Manchester	0161 832 5822
Middlesbrough	01642 243 026
Newcastle	01912 325 708
Nottingham	01159 476 407
Preston	01772 254 218
Sheffield	01142 723 301
Shrewsbury	01743 351 292
Stoke	01782 219 386
Swansea	01792 655 643
Wrexham	01978 266 033

Other RAF-related contacts

Air Cadets and Air Training Corps
Headquarters Air Cadets, RAF Newton, Nottinghamshire NG13 8HR.
Telephone: (switchboard) 01400 261 201 Fax: contact switchboard and request fax for Air Training Corps (do not abbreviate to ATC!).

University Air Squadrons
RAF College, Cranwell, Sleaford, Lincolnshire NG34 8HB.
Telephone: (switchboard) 01400 261 201 Fax: contact switchboard and request extension 7414, or dial 7414 (touch-tone phone) on hearing the pre-switchboard recorded message.

Royal Navy

If you require more details of a Royal Navy career, contact your nearest RN Careers Information Office from the following list. At the time of writing the existence of many of these offices is under review. If the number is unobtainable, write or telephone the Portsmouth number.

Director of Naval Recruitment, MoD, Victory Building,
HM Naval Base Portsmouth, Hampshire PO1 3LS.
Telephone: 01705 722 351 Fax: 01705 727 112

Town	Telephone
Aberdeen	01224 639 999
Belfast	01232 427 040
Birmingham	01216 334 995
Blackburn	01254 263 311
Brighton	01273 325 386
Bristol	0117 9260 233
Canterbury	01227 760 738
Cardiff	01222 726 813
Carlisle	0122 823 958
Chatham	01634 826 206
Chelmsford	01245 355 134
Coventry	01203 226 513
Croydon	0181 688 0489
Dorchester	01202 311 224
Glasgow	0141 221 6110
Guildford	01483 571 465
Hartlepool	01429 274 040
Ilford	0181 518 4565
Inverness	01463 233 668
Ipswich	01473 254 450
Leeds	0113 245 8195
Leicester	0116 262 0284
Lincoln	01522 525 661
Liverpool	0151 227 1764
London	0171 839 4643
Luton	0158 221 501
Manchester	0161 835 2916
Newcastle	0191 232 7048
Norwich	01603 620 033
Nottingham	0115 9419 503
Oxford	0186 553 431
Peterborough	0173 368 833
Plymouth	01752 266 487
Portsmouth	01705 826 536
Preston	01772 555 675
Redruth	01209 314 143
Sheffield	01142 721 476
Shrewsbury	01743 232 541
Southampton	01202 311 224
Stoke-on-Trent	01782 214 688

Swansea	01792 642 516
Watford	01923 244 055
Worcester	01905 723 677
Wrexham	01978 263 334

Pilot publications and equipment retailers

Aeronautical Information Service, NATS, AIS Central Office, First Floor, Control Tower Building, Heathrow Airport, Hounslow, Middlesex TW6 1JJ.
Telephone: 0181 745 3456 Fax: 0181 745 3453

Airlife Publishing Limited,
101 Longden Road, Shrewsbury, Shropshire SY3 9EB.
Telephone: 01743 235 651 Fax: 01743 232 944

Civil Aviation Authority Printing and Publications Services,
Grenville House, 37 Gratton Road, Cheltenham, Gloucestershire GL50 2BN.
Telephone: 01242 235 151 Fax: 01242 584 139

Civil Aviation Authority Publications also available to personal callers only at:
CAA Library, 45–49 Kingsway, London WC2B 6TE.
Telephone: 0171 379 7311 Fax: 0171 240 1153

Harry Mendelssohn Discount Sales,
49–51 Colinton Road, Edinburgh EH10 5DH.
Telephone: 0131 447 7777 Fax: 0131 452 9004

Inland Revenue (Claims Branch) – Piloting Transport Aircraft – Level 4 – NVQ Q1019882 Queries
Savings & Investments (Vocational Training Unit), St Johns House,
Merton Road, Bootle, Merseyside L69 9BB.
Telephone: 0151 472 6109 or 6110 or 6176 Fax: 0151 472 6006
(For pilots registered prior to July 1998)

Pooley's Aeroshopping (Shop), 16 New Quebec Street, London W1.
(Mail order) Elstree Aerodrome, Elstree, Hertfordshire WD6 3AW.
Telephone: (Shop) 0171 258 1468 (Mail Order) 0181 207 3749
Fax: 0181 953 2512

R D Aviation Limited,
25 Bankside, Kidlington, Oxford OX5 1JE.
Telephone: 01865 841 441 Fax: 01865 842 495

Transair Pilot Shops,
West Entrance, Fairoaks Airport, Chobham, Surrey GU24 8HX.
Telephone: 01276 858 533 Fax: 01276 855 464
50a Cambridge Street, London SW1V 4QQ.
Telephone: 0171 976 6787 Fax: 0171 233 6012

Contact addresses – aviation related

Acorne Sports Ltd, Wycombe Air Centre, Booker, Marlowe, Buckinghamshire SL7 3DR.
Telephone: 01494 451 703 or Fax: (for credit card orders) on 01494 465 456.

British Aerobatic Association Ltd., White Waltham Airfield, Nr. Maidenhead, Berkshire SL6 3NJ.
Telephone: 01455 617 211 Fax: 01455 250 271

British Balloon and Airship Club, 7 Llewellyn Road, Penllergaer, Swansea SA4 1BB.
Telephone: 01792 899 777 Fax: 01792 899 444

British Gliding Association, Kimberley House, Vaughan Way, Leicester LE1 4SE.
Telephone: 0116 2531 051 Fax: 0116 2515 939

British Hang Gliding & Parascending Association, The Old School Room, Loughborough Road, Leicester LE4 5PJ.
Telephone: 0116 261 1322 Fax: 0116 261 1323

British Microlight Aircraft Association, Bullring, Deddington, Oxfordshire OX5 4TT.
Telephone: 0186 9338 888 Fax: 0186 9337 116

British Parachute Association, Wharf Way, Glen Parva, Leicester LE2 9TF.
Telephone: 0116 2785 271 Fax: 0116 2477 662

British Womens Pilots Association, Rochester Airport, Chatham, Kent ME5 9SD.
Telephone: 01634 816 340 Fax: – no fax available

Civil Aviation Authority (General Enquiries)
See entry under **Contact addresses – private, commercial and airline pilots** (page 138).

General Aviation Awareness Council, c/o 50A Cambridge Street, London SW1V 4QQ.
Telephone: 0171 834 5631 Fax: 0171 834 8623

General Aviation Manufacturers & Traders Association (GAMTA), 19 Church Street, Brill, Aylesbury, Buckinghamshire HP18 9TG.
Telephone: 01844 238 020 Fax: 01844 238 087

Helicopter Club of Great Britain, Ryelands House, Aynho, Banbury, Oxfordshire OX17 3AT.
Telephone: 01869 810 646 Fax: 01869 810 755

International Air Tattoo Flying Scholarship for the Disabled – See details on page 52.

Popular Flying Association, Shoreham Airport, Shoreham, Sussex BN43 5FF.
Telephone: 01273 461 616 Fax: 01273 463 390

Royal Aero Club, Kimberley House, Vaughan Way, Leicester LE1 4SG.
Telephone: 0116 253 1051 Fax: 0116 251 5939

Glossary

(A)	Aeroplanes, when shown after PPL
AAC	Army Air Corps
ADF	Automatic Direction Finder
AEF	Air Experience Flight
AFI	Assistant Flying Instructor
AH	Artificial Horizon
AIS	Aeronautical Information Service
AME	Authorised Medical Examiner
AOPA	Aircraft Owners & Pilots Association
ASI	Air Speed Indicator
ATC	Air Traffic Control *or* Air Training Corps
ATPL	Airline Transport Pilot's Licence
BA	British Airways
BAe	British Aerospace
BCPL	Basic Commercial Pilot's Licence
BEA	British European Airways
BOAC	British Overseas Airways Corporation
CAA	Civil Aviation Authority
CAP	Civil Aviation Publication
CCF	Combined Cadet Force
CES	Cranwell Entry Standard
CFI	Chief Flying Instructor
COAT	College of Air Training
CPL	Commercial Pilot's Licence
CRT	Cathode Ray Tube (display)
DE	Direct Entry (Army Air Corps)
DI	Directional Indicator
ECG	Electrocardiograph
EFIS	Electronic Flight Instrumentation System
FAA	Federal Aviation Administration
FAI	Fédération Aéronautique Internationale
FCL	Flight Crew Licensing
FI	Flying Instructor
FRTO	Flight Radiotelephony Operator
FTS	Flying Training School
(G)	Gliders
GFT	General Flight Test
(H)	Helicopters, when shown after PPL
(hr)	Hour(s)

IAT	International Air Tattoo
ICAO	International Civil Aviation Organisation
IFR	Instrument Flight Rules
IMC	Instrument Meteorological Rating
IWR	Instrument Weather Rating
IR	Instrument Rating
JAA	Joint Aviation Authority
JAR	Joint Aviation Requirements
LOFT	Line Orientated Flying Training
MoD	Ministry of Defence
NATS	National Air Traffic Services
NCO	Non-commissioned officer
NFT	Navigation Flight Test
nm	Nautical mile(s), equivalent to 1.150 statute miles
NPA	Notice of Proposed Amendment
OASC	Officer and Aircrew Selection Centre
OATS	Oxford Air Training School
OCU	Operational Conversion Unit
ORD	Optional Retirement Date
PAYE	Pay as you earn
PIC	Pilot-in-Command
PPL	Private Pilot's Licence
QFE	'Q' Code for height above ground level
QFI	Qualified Flying Instructor
QNH	'Q' Code for height above sea level
RAeC	Royal Aero Club
Reg C	Regular Commission
RMAS	Royal Military Academy Sandhurst
RN(AS)	Royal Navy/Naval (Air Station)
RT	Radio Telephony
SRC	Special Regular Commission
SSC	Short Services (officers) Commission
STOVL	Short Take-off/Vertical Landing
T&S	Turn & Slip Indicator
TWU	Tactical Weapons Unit
UAS	University Air Squadron
UK	United Kingdom of Great Britain and Northern Ireland
U/S	Under Supervision
USA	United States of America
VAT	Value Added Tax
VDU	Visual Display Unit
VGS	Volunteer Gliding School
VHF	Very High Frequency
VOR	VHF Omni-directional Range
VR	Voluntary Reserve
VSI	Vertical Speed Indicator

Index